The Complete Guide to Facebook Advertising

Table of Contents

ACKNOWLEDGMENTS

I wanted to write this book after having multiple conversations with business owners who were often overwhelmed or confused when it comes to Facebook advertising. As I walked them through some of their options, I saw their eyes light up as they got excited about the possibilities for their businesses.

Writing this book was difficult, as Facebook updates its advertising platform on almost a weekly basis. Despite the many changes that I needed to track and document in this book, I was able to finally produce the 2020 edition of *The Complete Guide to Facebook Advertising*. Behind every great accomplishment stands a team. I want to thank the people responsible for helping me create this book.

Anne Felicitas, Editor: Thank you for all the long hours you spent researching, taking screenshots, and editing. You made this book perfect.

The AdvertiseMint Team: I am blessed to work with an amazing team that is dedicated to getting the very best results out of Facebook for our clients.

Our Facebook Representatives: Thank you for the endless explanations, video calls, and emails that help me and my team better understand the inner workings of Facebook's advertising platform. This book has the latest information, features, and strategies because of you.

Our Clients: It is an honor to be entrusted with the task of growing your business. The road to profitability is rarely a straight path, but I am grateful you have chosen us to be a part of your journey.

INTRODUCTION

I first began marketing back in college, using my cafeteria money to run paid search ads for a startup. Now, my team at AdvertiseMint and I have managed hundreds of millions of dollars in paid digital ads and have worked with brands such as Coca-Cola and Viacom.

I wrote this book because I wanted people to understand the power of Facebook ads and the available tools that help them both grow their businesses and spend less while reaching their ideal customers.

I update this book each year. It is always surprising to see the many changes to Facebook's advertising platform and exciting to think of the improvements that will come next.

When I spoke to readers about the earlier versions of this book, I heard conflicting reviews. Some said it was too advanced, others said it was too basic, many said it struck the perfect balance between challenging and easy. I read every review and tried to incorporate those critiques into the 2020 update. If you read the previous edition, you will find this new one includes concise walk-throughs, updated information (including changes to Ads Manager), and expert tips on the day-to-day duties of managing Facebook ads. My goal for this edition is to provide a comprehensive roadmap for anyone who wants to understand how Facebook advertising works and to show readers how to use Facebook's latest advertising tools in growing their businesses.

Before I get into more detail about Facebook advertising, I want to address a common misconception. Many new Facebook advertisers believe that Facebook is a magical platform that instantly generates millions of dollars overnight as though it were some lottery. This misconception often comes from teachers and mentors boasting about getting great results from Facebook ads in an attempt to persuade people to purchase their courses. Although it is possible to "win the Facebook lottery," Facebook advertising requires hard work to be successful. This is the common situation for many Facebook advertisers. When you run your Facebook ad campaigns, have patience and carefully tend to your ads.

FACEBOOK ADS HELP

The digital advertising landscape is subject to changes on any given day. This is not a task you can accomplish on your own. Advertising on Facebook has many moving parts: understanding your sales process, crafting your online ad funnel, creating highly engaging video content, and nailing the precise ad copy that will guide the online user from stranger to customer. It takes a team. If you want to scale your business to new heights in 2020, the AdvertiseMint team is here to help. To speak with one of our experienced and friendly representatives, contact us at:

844 236 4686 ext. 2
or
sales@advertisemint.com

FREE FACEBOOK AD TARGETING GUIDE

Download the 2020 version of our FREE printer-friendly Facebook ad targeting guide. Containing more than 850 targeting options, this guide will help you reach your ideal customers.

URL: **advertisemint.com/complete-guide-facebook-ad-targeting**

CHAPTER 1: WHY FACEBOOK

With Facebook, you can raise brand awareness among your ideal customers before they begin their product search. When they do look for the item they want to purchase, they will likely have your brand in mind. The benefits of Facebook advertising do not end here. There are three main reasons why every business should advertise on Facebook.

MOBILE, CONSUMER DATA, AND POWERFUL TOOLS

An Apple study found that iPhone users unlock their phones 80 times a day, confirming advertisers' long-held belief that people often shift attention to their mobile phones. Because consumers spend so much time on their mobile devices, it is important to bring your marketing messages to smartphones and in front of consumers. Facebook is the best way to reach consumers on mobile, thanks to its growing family of apps such as Instagram, WhatsApp, and Messenger.

Since the launch of the Facebook Pixel, Facebook's data now contains information on users' online behaviors, such as the apps they used, the websites they visited, and the amount of time they spent researching products. With this data you can target potential customers based on their purchase intent, previous interaction with your business, and so much more.

Facebook provides tools that allow you to strengthen relationships with customers no matter the size of your budget. Dynamic Product Ads, for example, show the exact item people viewed in an online product catalog. Dynamic Creatives, another ad type, instantly creates up to 4,000 ad variations to find the best combination that generates results. There are also Messenger bots, which offer businesses a way to automate conversations with customers on a large scale.

FACEBOOK REWARDS GOOD ADVERTISING PRACTICES

Facebook cares about its users. The company's mission statement vows to "give people the power to build community and bring the world closer together." However, Facebook cannot achieve that mission if users do not find the social networking platform valuable. To ensure users return to the app, Facebook prohibits annoying, disruptive, or irrelevant advertising practices from its platform by charging underperforming campaigns more than successful campaigns. If you hear anyone say, "Facebook ads don't work for me," it is likely due to the advertiser's need to create better ads.

For example, two competing smoothie shops are running Facebook ads. One smoothie shop runs lackluster, low-quality ads that are underperforming while the other runs engaging, entertaining, and educational ads that are instant hits with the target audience.

Facebook rewards the second smoothie shop with lower CPMs and CPCs because its performance proves to be valuable to users. As the ads of the first smoothie shop run continuously with no conversions, Facebook concludes that users find the ad to be repetitive and boring. Facebook penalizes the first smoothie shop with higher CPMs and CPCs.

Facebook measures the value of your ads using three tools: EdgeRank, an algorithm that determines which content is relevant to each user; Ad Relevance Score, a metric that measures your ad's relevance based on user engagement, video watch time, action rates, and feedback; and Customer Feedback Score, a rating that customers give your business after purchasing an item from your Facebook ad. When running ads on Facebook, always provide value to users.

CHAPTER 2: ACCOUNT SET-UP

To advertise on Facebook, you will need the following:

- Facebook user profile

- Facebook business page

- Facebook Pixel

- Billing set-up

- Instagram account (recommended)

- Business Manager account (recommended)

- Custom and Lookalike Audience (optional)

You need these elements to link your accounts across platforms and ensure that you are sending pixel data back to Facebook, which will help you improve your advertising results. Every Facebook profile comes with one ad account by default.

SETTING UP A FACEBOOK PROFILE

You likely have already completed this step, but if not, it is easy and takes only a few seconds. When you open a Facebook account, you will have the ability to create a business page and a Business Manager account, both of which are needed to run ads. Follow these steps to set up a Facebook profile:

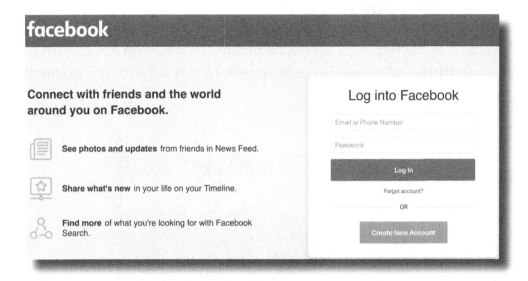

Step 1: Visit **https://www.facebook.com/**.

Step 2: Enter your name, email or phone number, password, birthday and gender.

Step 3: Verify your email or phone number.

SETTING UP A BUSINESS PAGE

The next step is creating a Facebook business page, which is required to run ads. All the ads you run will appear in the Ad Library under the name of your business page.

Step 1: Visit **https://www.facebook.com/pages/**.

Step 2: Click **Create Page**.

Step 3: Choose page type.

Choose the page type that represents your entity. If you own a business or a brand, choose "Business or Brand." If you are using your page to connect with your community, group, organization, team, or club, then choose "Community or Public Figure."

Step 4: Add page name and category.

When choosing your category, write a word or two that best describes your page. When you type in the first keyword, a dropdown list of options will automatically appear.

Step 5: Save information.

SETTING UP BUSINESS MANAGER

If you plan to manage only a single ad account and business page, you can continue without Business Manager; otherwise, you must sign up for an account.

Sign Up for Business Manager

https://business.facebook.com

You will use Business Manager to manage all of your assets for Facebook advertising, such as pages, accounts, and product catalogs. After you create your business account, you will need to transfer any assets you want to manage under that account. The most common are pages, other ad accounts, and Instagram accounts.

FACEBOOK PIXEL INSTALLATION

The Facebook Pixel is a JavaScript code that measures, optimizes, and builds an audience for your ad campaigns. There are three main benefits of using the pixel. First, you can use the pixel's data to create a Custom Audience. Second, you can use the Custom Audience data, which provides never-before-seen information on website visitors' demographics, interests, and purchase behaviors, as a secondary resource to Google Analytics or other analytics services. Third, you can use the pixel's data and Dynamic Product Ads to remarket to visitors who visited specific pages of your site.

Each Facebook user has a Facebook ID. When installed on your website, the pixel tracks users' IDs and compiles data on website visits and actions. By having this digital footprint, you can customize your ad campaigns to be more effective. If you want to view your Facebook ID, visit **https://findmyfbid.com/** and enter the name of your Facebook profile. To create a Facebook pixel, follow these steps:

Step 1: Visit **https://www.facebook.com/events_manager**.

Step 2: Under Data Sources, click **Add New Data Source** and select **Facebook Pixel**.

Step 3: Name your pixel.

Step 4: Connect or install the pixel to your website.

There are three ways to connect your pixel to your website:

Method A: Add Code Using Partner Integration

Use this step if you are using a popular platform such as Squarespace, WordPress, or Shopify. You will select your CMS and follow instructions on how to add the pixel.

Method B: Manually Add Pixel Code to Website

You will copy and paste the pixel directly above the </head> tag on your website header. Turn on the Advanced Matching feature before copying the pixel code, as this helps deliver additional site visitor information, such as name, email, or phone number.

Method C: Email Instructions to Developer

If you do not know HTML, choose the third option to send the code and the instructions for implementing the pixel to your website developer.

Step 5: Test your pixel.

Once you install the pixel, you can use two methods to test whether it is working. The first appears on the Install Pixel page. After you install the pixel, add your URL and press **Send Test Traffic**. The screen will display "Active Message" if the pixel is firing correctly. The second option is using the Pixel Helper Extension for Google Chrome, which will indicate whether a pixel is active on a website.

Step 5: Add events you wish to track. (Advanced)

Events are actions users take on your website, such as viewing products, adding items to cart, and purchasing. With events, you can show ads to people who have completed an action, such as adding to cart without purchasing. The events will fire only after users take action on specific pages. If you use platforms such as Shopify, WooCommerce, or Magento, the important events are already coded into your site. If you have a custom website, you may need to manually enter the events you want to track. For this, you can use Google Tag Manager or hire a developer to do the job.

AD ACCOUNT BILLING

To run ads, you must add a billing method to your Ads Manager account. You can do this by visiting

www.facebook.com/ads/manager/account_settings/account_billing

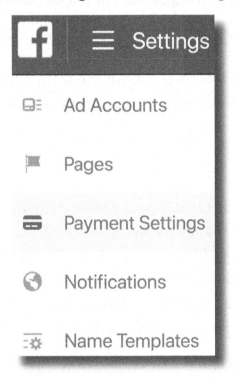

First, click the **Add Payment Method** button. From there enter your credit card, debit card, or Paypal information, or log in to your bank and sync your account and routing numbers with Facebook.

On the Ad Account Billing page, you will also find your account spending limit. This is the amount you are willing to spend on Facebook ads. Reference this tool to ensure you do not overspend on your ad budget. You will need to continually update this number; otherwise, all of your ads will pause when the amount is reached. You can change, remove, or reset this number at any time.

SETTING UP CUSTOM AND LOOKALIKE AUDIENCES

While it is not mandatory to begin advertising, it is generally recommended to spend some time creating any custom and lookalike audiences for your account. Custom audiences should include any customer lists, lifetime value lists, email lists, past or current leads, website visitors, landing page visitors, pixel events like add to cart and purchases, or individuals who have watched your videos or engaged with your business via social media. You will need custom audiences if you want to target your ads, exclude from targeting, or create lookalike audiences. You will generally want to create lookalike audiences based on your end goal. If purchases are your goal, create a lookalike of your customers. If you want app installs, create a lookalike based on people who downloaded your app. Although lookalikes can range from 1% to 10% in size, most advertisers on Facebook should focus on the 1% lookalikes to begin with and expand to larger sizes only after they exhaust their audience. Lookalikes built off dynamic data, like purchase events via the pixel, will generally perform better than a static list of uploaded customers.

To create audiences, visit: **www.facebook.com/adsmanager/audiences**

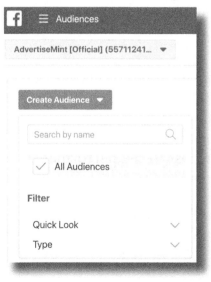

FACEBOOK BOOSTED AND INSTAGRAM PROMOTED POSTS

Facebook Boosted Posts are regular posts that you publish on your business page and pay to show to an audience with the targeting that you define. Whereas regular posts appear only once to your followers' News Feeds, boosted posts appear to a target audience you choose, even an audience that is not your followers. Like an ad, boosted posts will repeatedly appear in your audience's feed for the amount of time that you choose. Instagram also has a boosted feature that works similarly to Facebook's. It is called promoted posts. To boost a Facebook post, you must publish a status update on your Facebook page and pay Facebook to turn it into an ad. This process is similar for Instagram.

Boosting a post is the fastest and easiest way to begin running ads. Because boosted posts do not have all the features that come with ads created through Ads Manager, boosted posts are best only for beginners.

BOOSTING A FACEBOOK POST

Step 1: Upload an image or video to your fan page. Click **Boost Post**.

Step 2: Enter the time you want the ad to run and the details for targeting.

Step 3: Enter your budget and billing details.

Step 4: Click **Publish**.

Step 5: Return to the post to see performance on reach, engagement, views, and clicks.

PROMOTING AN INSTAGRAM POST

Step 1: Sign up for an **Instagram Business Account**.

Step 2: Publish a video or image.

Step 3: Click **Promote**.

Step 4: Connect your Instagram account to your Facebook business page.

Step 5: Fill in the details for objective, target audience, budget, and duration.

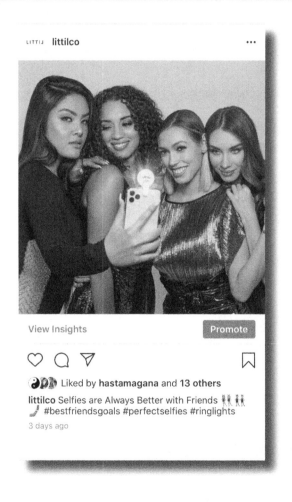

CHAPTER 3: ADS CREATION IN ADS MANAGER

Ads Manager is the dashboard where you can create, edit, and view all of your ads that are running across Facebook, Instagram, Messenger, and the Audience Network. The core of Facebook advertising, Ads Manager, is the recommended location from which to create your ads.

Facebook recently redesigned the structure of Ads Manager, which is broken down by three levels: the campaign level, the ad set level, and the ads level. You will need to have all three elements active in order to begin running your ads. This chapter walks you through all the elements currently available in Ads Manager.

CAMPAIGNS

Campaigns are the first thing you will need when creating your Facebook ads. In the campaign level, you can choose the objective of your ads, name your campaign, enable split testing, and choose your campaign budget optimization.

Guided Creation vs Quick Creation

Before you create your ads, you have the option to use the quick creation or guided creation workflows. These two options contain two different visual layouts, although the information you select for each ad remains the same. With quick creation, which is the default, advanced choice, you can create parts of your ad to complete later, and you can create your ads non-sequentially. Guided creation is the older format that may be easier for beginners. You can switch between these two workflows at any time during the ad creation process.

BUYING TYPE: AUCTION VS REACH AND FREQUENCY

Before your choose your objective, you must choose between buying your ads in the auction or through reach and frequency.

Auction: This is the most common option that many advertisers use. You will compete with other advertisers in the top spot of users' feeds. Choose the auction if you plan to run small, ongoing tests.

Reach and frequency: With this type of bidding, you can pre-approve the price you want to pay to reach your audience. Once you select your audience and the dates you want your ads to run, you can then enter in CPMs, which, once approved, will be locked in and utilized during the length of the campaign. Use reach and frequency if you want to lock in prices over the length of the campaign or when you want to pay the lowest price to ensure you reach a highly valuable audience. You can use reach and frequency with the brand awareness, reach, traffic, engagement, app installs, video views, and conversion objectives.

SPECIAL AD CATEGORY

In 2018, Facebook made changes to employment, credit, and housing ads when ProPublica revealed in an article that advertisers could use ad targeting to exclude people of certain ethnic groups from seeing employment, credit, or housing ads, which is illegal in the United States.

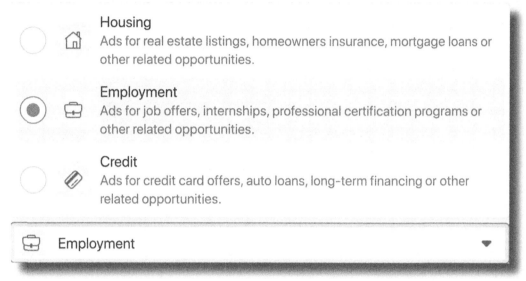

The special ad category tool will limit some ad targeting capabilities to prevent unlawful discrimination and to ensure you follow Facebook's ad policies. If you want to run credit, employment, or housing ads, you must select the correct category before creating your campaign. Once selected, some of your ad targeting options will be removed. For example, you will not be able to target users based on their ethnicity when running housing ads.

Credit: Ads that promote or link to credit card offers, auto loans, personal loan services, business loan services, mortgage loans, and long term financing.

Employment Opportunity: Ads that promote or link to a full-time or part-time employment opportunity, internships, professional certification programs, job boards, job fairs, or ads detailing perks a company may provide.

Housing Opportunity: Ads that promote or link to listings for the sale or rental of a home or apartment, homeowners insurance, mortgage insurance, home equity, or appraisal services.

CHOOSING YOUR OBJECTIVE

Objectives, which define the goals you want your ad to achieve, are extremely important. They will change the behavior of Facebook's system when showing ads to users and the features that appear on Ads Manager's three campaign levels.

Always choose the final business outcome as your objective. If you own an e-commerce business and you aim to increase sales, you could choose brand awareness, traffic, engagement, or video views as your objective, but Facebook would view your final outcome (a sale) as a conversion since you are finding people who will complete a purchase. Here is an example: You own an online pet store targeting men in New York who like dogs. Your audience is composed of three individuals:

Tom: Likes dogs. Uses only Instagram. Purchases three dog products every week.

Sam: Likes dogs. Loves watching dog videos. Purchases one dog product every month.

Joe: Loves dogs. Uses Facebook every day. Clicks ads featuring dogs but never buys online.

Facebook needs to determine who between the three is the best person to show the ad. If you choose the reach objective, Facebook would focus on reaching all three individuals. If you choose the traffic objective, Facebook would show the ad to Joe first, since he clicks on every ad, and will not likely click yours. If you choose the video views objective, Facebook would show the ad to Sam first, since he watches a lot of dog videos. With the conversions objective, Facebook would show the ad to Tom first because he often buys similar dog products online.

Facebook matches the right user with the right ad at the right time. As a result, ads feel less like ads and more like native, organic content that users like to see in their feeds. This process happens behind the scenes. Your only job is to select the right objective.

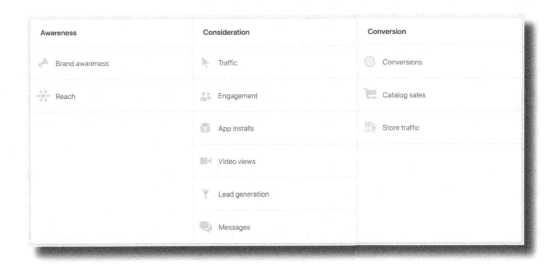

Awareness	Consideration	Conversion
Brand awareness	Traffic	Conversions
Reach	Engagement	Catalog sales
	App installs	Store traffic
	Video views	
	Lead generation	
	Messages	

AWARENESS OBJECTIVES

- **Brand Awareness:** The brand awareness objective increases consumers' brand recall of your ads. This objective is often used by larger brands such as Geiko, Old Spice, and Coca-Cola.

- **Reach:** The reach objective allows you to select an audience and control the number of times your ad appears in front of that audience. Use this objective if you want to reach a large percentage of your audience on a specific day, for example, the day before an election, or if you want more control over the number of times your ad appears to users.

CONSIDERATION OBJECTIVES

- **Traffic:** The traffic objective focuses on finding users who will click a link to your landing page or website. Although getting people to your website may seem like a good choice, Facebook does not view this as a valid business objective since people who often click on ads do not necessarily complete critical business objectives, such as completing a purchase.

- **Engagement:** The engagement objective focuses on finding users who are highly likely to engage with your page, content, or event, for example, liking your page or RSVPing to an event.

- **App Installs:** The app installs objective increases the downloads of your mobile app.

- **Video Views:** The video views objective reaches individuals who have high average video-views times while on Facebook or Instagram.

- **Lead Generation:** The lead generation objective unlocks Lead Ads that allow you to collect users' information directly inside

Facebook's app or website.

- **Messages:** The messages objective sends users to automated conversations managed by bots on Messenger. The bots answer questions customers might have about your business.

OBJECTIVES: CONVERSION

- **Conversions:** The conversion objective finds individuals who are most likely to complete specific actions on your website, such as viewing a page, adding to cart, or completing a purchase. This is the most popular objective for generating revenue.

- **Catalog Sales:** The catalog sales objective unlocks the ability to create Dynamic Product Ads (DPAs), which are ads created automatically after a user performs a specific action. DPAs are available for e-commerce, automotive, travel, and real estate businesses.

- **Store Traffic:** The store traffic objective drives nearby customers to a local retail store.

Before you create a Facebook ad, know your campaign objective. Do you want to send people to your brick-and-mortar store? Do you want more brand exposure? Do you want more sales? Facebook wants you to choose an objective before creating your ad because different objectives have different eligible ad placements and formats. For example, only an ad with the objective store visits can feature an ad with a map that directs customers to your location.

SPLIT TESTING (VARIABLES AND NUMBER OF AD SETS)

Split testing allows you to test different elements of your ad campaigns to gain valuable insights about the performance of your ads. When you enable split testing, Facebook will automatically split your audience into different groups. Each group will contain a different ad variable, and the results will be displayed during and after the test so you can see which version of the ad performs the best.

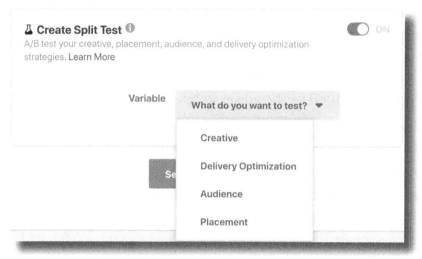

You can test the following variables:

Creative: This includes elements such as images, image color, video style, video format, video length, video thumbnail, videos versus images, or different ad units.

Delivery Optimization: This allows you to test different delivery optimization metrics, such as bidding, budgets, and delivery.

Audience: This allows you to test different audience segments to see which one has the highest performance.

Placement: This enables you to test which placements (News Feeds, Stories, Watch, Marketplace, Audience Network, etc.) provide the best return.

CAMPAIGN BUDGET OPTIMIZATION

Underneath the list of objectives, you will also notice an option to enable campaign budget optimization (CBO). With this feature, you are allowing the system to control the budget at the campaign level rather than at the ad set level. Meaning, the algorithm will distribute the total budget to the ad sets according to each ad's performance. CBO saves time by automating the process of individually entering your daily budget for each ad set. It also allows the system to allocate the most money to the best-performing ad.

CBO is currently your campaigns' default setting. In the past, your ad budget was controlled in the ad set level. With the budget CBO moved to the campaign level, Facebook can automatically adjust the ad budgets for any active ad sets inside the campaign, driving the lowest possible cost for your objective. Think of it as an autopilot feature that ensures you are getting the best return on your ad spend.

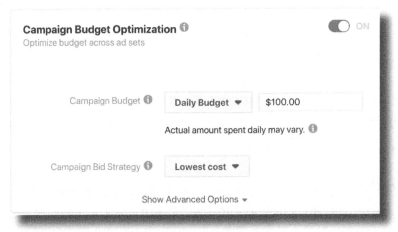

Once you enable CBO, you must choose between a daily budget and a lifetime budget, then pick a bid strategy. Bid strategies are options that determine how Facebook will spend your money in a way that is optimized to get your desired results. There are four options:

Lowest Cap: This option will get the most results for your budget. Facebook will find users who will complete your objective at the lowest possible price. This is the most common bidding method and the default choice when creating your campaign. This option gives Facebook the ability to automatically raise or lower your bid, run the ad at optimal times, and find users who will complete your objective. Unfortunately, sometimes you may experience low delivery with this method because your bids are not high enough to compete with other advertisers.

Cost Cap: This allows you to control your costs while getting the most results for your budget. For example, if you indicate you want to pay $1 per app install, Facebook will charge you $1 per result. However, the charge may fluctuate when your budget increases or decreases.

Bid Cap: This allows you to control your bid in each auction. The target amount per action must be entered. This bidding strategy will focus only on bids that are lower than your bid cap amount. For example, you may bid $50, but if the highest bid below yours is $20, then you would pay only the next highest amount to win the $20 bid—for example, $20.01.

The best way to find what bidding option works best for your company is to test them. For reference, the most popular bidding strategy is cost cap and lowest cost.

AD SETS

At the ad sets level, you can choose your conversion events, dynamic creative, audience, placements, budget, and schedule.

Audience Size and Estimated Daily Results

On the right column of the ad set level are two critical tools that update as you make changes to your audience, placements, or budget.

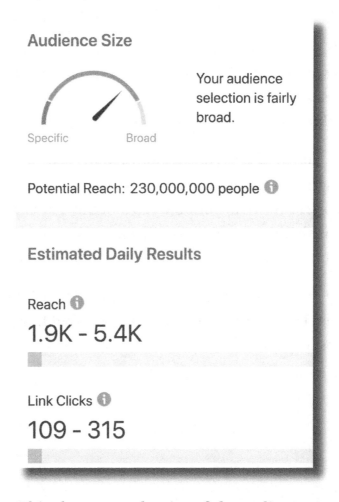

Audience Size: This shows you the size of the audience you selected. If you select an audience that is too broad, you may quickly exhaust your budget, and your ads will struggle to remain relevant to users. If you select an audience that is too specific, you may run out of users to target and struggle to expand. Most advertisers will have a variety of ad sets, some with large audiences and some with small audiences. If an ad set is not reaping the desired results, you must make changes in the ad set level.

Estimated Daily Results: A tool that updates as you increase or decrease your budget, this provides an estimate of the number of users your ads will reach. It also provides an estimated number of conversions using a seven-day click, one-day view attribution window. This is a handy tool when you want to know the type of results to expect. Once you enter a budget, Facebook will report an estimate of the results your ad will generate.

AD SET NAME (NAMING TEMPLATES)

Naming your ad sets is important in keeping your campaign structure well organized. Use a naming structure that includes the audience you are targeting; demographics, such as age, gender, or location; placements, and bid strategies. You must name your ad sets consistently as your account grows so your team can quickly find reports and make the necessary changes. Facebook has a tool called naming templates, accessible from the sprocket icon next to Ad Set Name.

This feature allows you to automatically use elements from your ad campaigns and ad sets in your naming structure. The list of available options is below:

- Campaign ID
- Campaign Name
- Objective
- Ad Set ID
- Ad Set Updated Date
- Age
- City
- Country
- Custom Audiences (Excluded)
- Custom Audiences (Included)
- Gender
- Interests
- Mobile Device
- Mobile Operating System
- ZIP Code
- Custom Text

There is also an additional formatting option that allows you to separate each field with a dash or a comma.

DELIVERY

The delivery section shows your conversion locations, pixel events, optimization for ad delivery, the allocated conversion window, your bidding method, and charging method.

Conversion Event Location

Conversion Event

The conversion event is what Facebook will optimize for. You can select from different conversion events based on what has been set up with your pixel. The conversion event is typically the end action you want your users to take after seeing your ads.

OPTIMIZATION FOR AD DELIVERY

Your choice of optimization for ad delivery will affect who sees your ad. This is where ad budgets and the learning phase come into play. Facebook wants to see 50 conversion events per ad set per week to optimize ad delivery. This means if you own an e-commerce store that receives fewer than 50 purchases per week, the recommended action is to either increase your ad budget or move your ad delivery optimization one level back to add to cart, landing page views, or clicks to ensure you are hitting those 50 conversion events per week. Unfortunately, going back a level on your conversion events will prompt Facebook to optimize your ads based on people who click rather than people who purchase. If you are not reaching the 50 conversion events per week, then your ad set will slowly stop delivering because Facebook does not have adequate data to optimize your delivery.

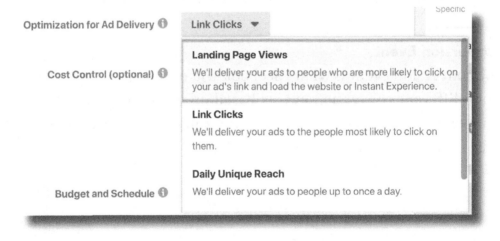

CONVERSION WINDOW

The conversion window is the length of time you wish to wait before counting a conversion.

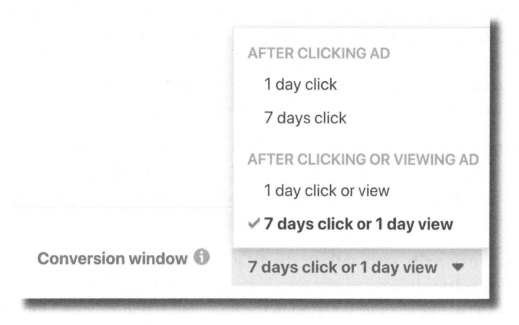

You have four options:

- One day after clicking an ad

- Seven days after clicking an ad

- One day after clicking or viewing an ad

- Seven days after clicking or viewing an ad

The conversion window you choose depends on your preference. If you are strict on your attribution, one day after clicking an ad is the best option. If you choose this option, however, your ad will not receive credit for a conversion event if a user does not immediately purchase within the one-day window. On the other end of the spectrum is seven days after clicking or one day after viewing an ad. Using this option, Facebook will count an event as a conversion if a user viewed or clicked on your ad a week ago and converted from a different ad or advertising platform, such as Google or a third-party site.

Multi-touch attribution is the process of determining which step of the customer journey led to the final purchase. Last-touch attribution can be misleading because it gives all of the credit to the last ad a user clicked.

When selecting your options, the default and recommended window is seven-days click or one-day view because they account for a wider view of the ad and the role it played in the final conversion. Having a longer conversion window also allows you to collect more data for the learning phase.

COST CONTROL

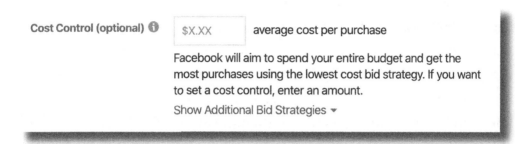

Setting a cost control is optional. You should set one if you have a target cost per result. If you leave this blank, Facebook's system will spend your budget and try to get you the most results. Setting up cost control tells Facebook which results to spend your budget on. Certain cost controls become available with certain objectives. For example, you can cap your costs with the objectives traffic, engagement, and app installs.

DELIVERY TYPE: ACCELERATED

By default, your ad campaigns will utilize "pacing," a process in which Facebook shows your ads to users evenly over the course of the day. If you need to run your ads or reach full delivery at a specific time, select the accelerated delivery option, which will spend your budget as quickly as possible. A word of caution: The accelerated delivery will exhaust your budget. Facebook has 1.6 billion daily active users, and accelerating your budget can often result in your entire daily budget being spent in a matter of minutes. Use accelerated delivery only when advertising during short-term special events, for example, promoting a sale the morning of Black Friday or reaching spectators at Dodger's Stadium during a game.

Delivery Type ⓘ

• **Standard (Recommended)**
Get results throughout your selected schedule

Accelerated
Spend your budget and get results as quickly as possible

BIDDING STRATEGIES

When you advertise on Facebook, you can control your budget to maximize cost-efficiency while maintaining your business goals. Facebook has three bidding strategies available: cost cap, bid cap, and target cost.

Objective	Bid Control	Cost Control
Reach	Bid cap	
Traffic		Cost cap, bid cap
Engagement		Cost cap, bid cap
App Installs		Cost cap, bid cap
Video Views		Cost cap, bid cap
Lead Generation		Cost cap, bid cap, target cost
Messages	Bid cap	
Conversions		Cost cap, bid cap, target cost
Catalog Sales		Cost cap, bid cap, and target cost
Store Visits		Bid cap

DYNAMIC CREATIVE

Dynamic creative allows you to upload multiple ad elements (images, videos, titles, descriptions, and CTAs) and automatically generate every possible combination of those assets.

Once you enable dynamic creative, Facebook's delivery system will mix and match your ad elements to find the combinations that perform the best. Up to 4,000 ad variations can be created using this tool. With this tool enabled, you can quickly find the version of the ad that garners the best results. Note that you can have only one dynamic creative ad per ad set.

BUDGET AND SCHEDULE

The budget and schedule tool gives you full control over the exact days and times you want your ads to run. You can choose between daily budget and lifetime budget.

Daily Budget (Recommended)

This option, using the pacing delivery method, will spend your entire daily budget over the course of the day. You must select a start date and either let the ad run indefinitely or set an end date. As you update your daily budget, make sure to reference the Estimate Daily Results chart to see estimates on the number of results that will be generated with that budget.

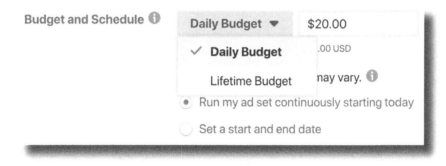

LIFETIME BUDGET

Using the lifetime budget, you must select a start and end date, as well as the total ad budget to be used during that period of time. Facebook will spend the allocated budget by the end date.

When you enable lifetime budgets, you unlock the Ad Scheduling, or Day Parting, feature, which allows you to run ads only on specific days and at specific times. For example, you can use Ad Scheduling when inviting local residents to join your bar's happy hour. This feature is especially beneficial to retail businesses or for lead generation during hours when the sales team is active.

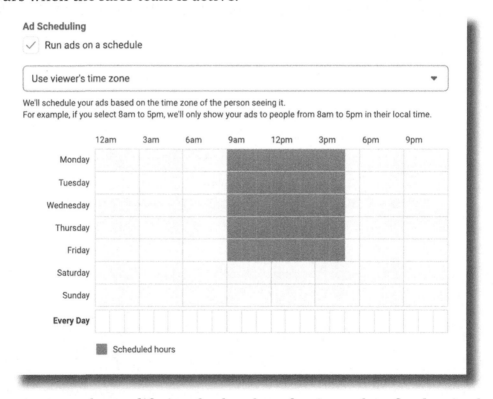

You can extend your lifetime budget by selecting a date further in the future and increasing the total ad budget.

CUSTOM AUDIENCES

Custom Audiences is one of Facebook's most powerful advertising tools, allowing you to target users who are already in your customer list or have previously interacted with your business on Facebook by clicking on your ad or following your business page. Users in your Custom Audience are typically more likely to be interested in your business. Targeting such an audience will improve your ad quality score because the ads will most likely be relevant to the users you are reaching. The most successful ad campaigns usually target Custom Audiences.

You can select one or more Custom Audiences or Lookalike Audiences. Any additional ad targeting you select, such as interests and behaviors, will be applied to the individuals inside the Custom or Lookalike Audiences you uploaded. You can also exclude Custom Audiences from your ad targeting. This allows you to remove certain audience segments from receiving your ads. You can, for example, exclude customers who opted out of your email marketing campaigns. When running a sale for an item, you can exclude customers who recently purchased the product for the full price.

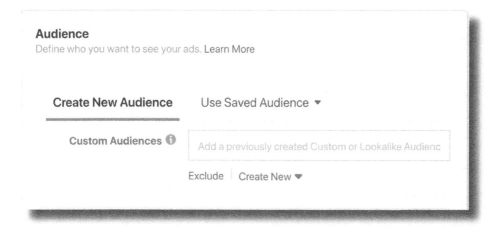

CREATING CUSTOM AUDIENCES

There are 10 types of Custom Audiences, which are divided into two categories: your sources and Facebook's sources.

Your Sources

- **Website Traffic (Up to 180 Days):** Everyone who visited your website, only users who visited specific pages of your website, visitors who took specific actions on your site, and visitors who spent a certain amount of time on your website.

- **App Activity (Up to 180 Days):** Users who opened your app, most active users, users who purchased a certain amount from your app, and users in specific audience segments.

- **Customer List:** Individuals in your list of leads, individuals with a customer lifetime value, individuals without a customer lifetime value, and leads imported from MailChimp.

- **Offline Activity:** People who interacted with your business offline, such as visiting your retail store or calling your business number.

Facebook Sources

- **Video (up to 365 days):** Users who watched 3 or 10 seconds of your video, users who watched 25%, 50%, 75%, or 100% of your video, and who completed or watched at least 15 seconds of your video (ThruPlay).

- **Lead Forms (up to 90 days):** Users who filled out or opened your lead form on Facebook or Instagram, who opened but did not submit a form, and who opened and submitted a form.

- **Instant Experience (up to 365 days):** Users who opened your Instant Experience ad and who clicked any link in your Instant Experience ad.

- **Instagram (up to 365 days):** Everyone who engaged with your business on Instagram, who visited your business profile, who engaged with your post or ad, who sent a message to your business profile, and who saved your post or ad.

- **Events (up to 365 days):** Users who RSVPed as "going" or "interested," who visited the event page, who engaged with the event page or tickets, who purchased tickets, and who intend to purchase tickets.

- **Facebook Pages (up to 365 days):** Everyone who engaged with or visited your page, who engaged with your post or ad on Facebook, who clicked any call-to-action button on your page, who sent a message to your page, and who saved your page or page posts.

LOOKALIKE AUDIENCES

With Lookalike Audiences, you can find people similar to those in your Custom Audience. To create Lookalikes, you will need to select the Lookalike source, which can be any Custom Audience; indicate a location by continent, region, or county; and choose an audience size, which can range from 1% to 10% of your selected area. For example, if you selected a customer list and a 1% Lookalike for the United States, the Lookalike will include the 1% of individuals in the United States who most closely resemble your source audience.

When selecting a Lookalike source, you will have the option to use value-based sources. Traditional Lookalikes place equal value on the individuals inside the Custom Audience you uploaded and find more people like those individuals. However, if you have a Custom Audience that includes the total amount spent by each customer, you can create a Lifetime Value Lookalike Audience that gives more weight to individuals who have spent more money on your business and less to those who made smaller purchases.

Facebook does not disclose how it determines an audience to be a Lookalike, but the system most likely searches for similarities in personal interests, demographics, websites visited, purchase behavior, and searches performed on Facebook.

After Cambridge Analytica, Facebook removed many ad-targeting options. Although those options are no longer available to advertisers, Facebook still internally monitors and tracks important data, which advertisers can still access using Lookalike Audiences.

SAVED AUDIENCES

Rather than creating new audiences each time, you can reuse a previously created audience and upload it to other ad sets. You can do that by clicking the "Save This Audience" button at the bottom of the page and giving it a name. This audience will be saved under your "Audiences" tab and appear on the ad set level when you are uploading audiences to your targeting. Alternatively, you can also duplicate ad sets, copying all the ad targeting into the new ad set.

LOCATIONS

Targeting the right location can be critical to the success of your ads. Facebook gives you several options to ensure you are targeting the best location for your business.

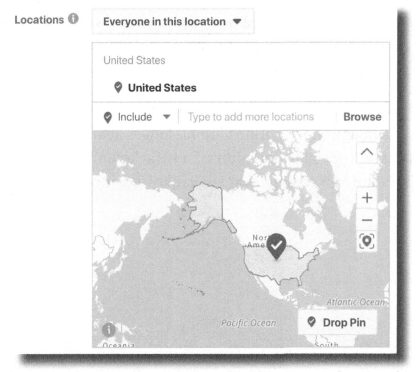

When setting the location in the ad set level, you can choose who in the location you want to target. You have four options:

Everyone in this location: This recommended option includes users whose home address is listed in the area and users who were recently in the location.

People who live in this location: This includes only users whose home address is listed in the selected location.

People recently in this location: This includes only users who are or were recently in the location.

People traveling in this location: This includes only users who are or were recently in the location but whose home address is more than 125 miles away.

You can also select an area that you want to include or exclude from your ads. These options include:

- Continents
- Countries
- DMA / Market
- ZIP Codes / Postal Codes
- States / Provinces
- Cities (Current City Only or 10- to 50-Mile Radius)
- Neighborhood
- Street Addresses
- Airport (1- to 50-Mile Radius)
- Dropped Pin (1- to 50-Mile Radius)

You also have the ability to add locations in bulk, which requires an Excel or CSV file with the correct data.

AGE, GENDER, AND LANGUAGES

Although you can target users from age 13 to age 65 and beyond, you must ensure that the age you choose does not violate Facebook's ad policies and local laws. For example, if you are advertising a dating app, do not target users who are below the age of 18.

The default language is the language of the browser or mobile device that the user is using when accessing Facebook or Instagram. You can leave the option for language blank, but you should add the language of the users you want to target.

DETAILED TARGETING

Targeting your ads correctly is essential to succeeding in Facebook advertising. Do not let the tiny detailed targeting box fool you. There are hundreds of targeting options within. You can target individuals based on demographics, interests, and behaviors. Make sure to download *The Complete Guide to Facebook Ad Targeting* to view the main ad targeting options.

https://www.advertisemint.com/complete-guide-facebook-ad-targeting-signup/

Detailed Targeting ⓘ   Include people who match ⓘ

    Add demographics, interes | Suggestions | **Browse**

Exclude People

    Expand your detailed targeting to reach more people when it's likely to improve performance.

Learn more about detailed targeting expansion.

Take some time to research and review the available options. As Facebook advertising has evolved throughout the years, many targeting options have been removed or replaced. Depending on your business, this change may cause issues with reaching your ideal customers. There are numerous ways you can mix and match your targeting options, which fit into three categories:

Single Targeting: You can target a single audience to reach anyone who meets your criteria. For example, you can target a single interest, such as dogs, to serve ads to users who like dogs.

Multiple Targeting: You can combine targeting options to create a broader criteria. For example, you can target anyone who likes dogs or cats. Users who like dogs or cats will see the ad.

Narrow Audience: You can reduce your audience size by including multiple targeting options. For example, you can target individuals who like dogs but narrow the audience to also include those who like cats. Only specific individuals who like both dogs and cats will see the ad.

Exclude: You can exclude an audience from your targeting. For example, you can target individuals who like dogs and exclude those who like birds from seeing your ads.

Mastering ad targeting is an essential element of Facebook advertising. There is no perfect combination that always works. You must test your targeting to determine which segments produce the best results for your business.

EXPANDED TARGETING

Facebook is always trying to help you reach the right customer at the right time. To accomplish this, the company launched a feature called Expanded Targeting.

 Expand your detailed targeting to reach more people when it's likely to improve performance.

Although it is the default option, you can still disable Expanded Targeting. When enabled, it will show your ads to individuals outside of your ad targeting if the system believes it will reach your objective within your bidding strategy. For example, if you are showing your ads to people who have an interest in dogs and cats, Facebook may show your ads to people who are interested in pets, hamsters, or fish because those who like dogs and cats are likely to be animal lovers.

Because Facebook has more targeting options than you can imagine, using Expanded Targeting can improve your campaigns. However, in some cases, when this feature is enabled, your audience size and spend may increase without reaping the desired results. You must test the feature to see if it works for your business. As Facebook continues to improve its technology, Expanded Targeting should become more efficient in finding and reaching the right customers at the right time.

CONNECTIONS

The Connections tool targets individuals who are connected with one of your properties on Facebook, for example, your business pages, your apps, or your events.

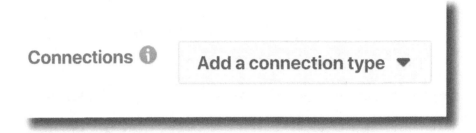

Your options for the Connections tool are the following:

- People who like your page

- Friends of people who like your page

- Exclude people who like your page

- People who used your app

- Friends of people who used your app

- Exclude people who used your app

- People who responded to your event

- Exclude people who already responded to your event

- Advanced combinations

These targeting options are not as popular as audience or interest targeting, but they can be used in situations where you want to reach or exclude a specific audience or reach people who are friends of the people you wish to reach.

PLACEMENTS

Placements are the areas where your ads will appear, which can include Facebook, Instagram, Messenger, WhatsApp, and the Audience Network. Make sure the placement you choose supports your ad format because each placement has certain restrictions for ad size, video length, and ad copy.

Automatic placements, which is the default option, will show your ads across all of Facebook's properties to reach your audience at the lowest possible price. For example, if a person you are targeting uses Instagram Stories and Facebook Marketplace regularly, Facebook may show your ad on Marketplace first because the auction cost for Marketplace is lower than Instagram Stories. Facebook recommends using all placements because there are more opportunities to reach your target audience at a lower price.

On the other hand, some placements often become expensive, depending on the results you want to generate. The type of business you own and the individuals you are targeting will affect the cost of your placements. If you are new to Facebook advertising, use automatic placements. If you are an advanced Facebook advertiser and are optimizing your return on ad spend, then you should review the cost per result by placement and make adjustments to ensure that you are maximizing your return.

Placements

Show your ads to the right people in the right places.

- **Automatic Placements (Recommended)**

  Use automatic placements to maximize your budget and help show your ads to more people. Facebook's delivery system will allocate your ad set's budget across multiple placements based on where they're likely to perform best. Learn More

- **Edit Placements**

  Manually choose the places to show your ad. The more placements you select, the more opportunities you'll have to reach your target audience and achieve your business goals. Learn More

There are currently 14 placement options available:

- Facebook Desktop and Mobile News Feeds
- Instagram Feed
- Facebook Marketplace
- Facebook Video Feeds
- Facebook Right Column
- Instagram Explore
- Messenger Inbox
- Instagram Stories
- Facebook Stories
- Messenger Stories
- Facebook Instream Videos
- Messenger Sponsored Messages
- Facebook Instant Articles
- Audience Network: partner apps and websites, native, banner, interstitial, rewarded videos, and in-stream videos

Placements may or may not become available based on the objective you select when creating your campaign. Options that are not in the list but that Facebook is currently testing include Facebook search and groups. Those tests may or may not roll out in the coming months.

SPECIFIC MOBILE DEVICES AND OPERATION SYSTEMS, ONLY WI-FI

As an advertiser, you can target users based on specific mobile devices. This is essential if you are a mobile app developer or an individual selling accessories for specific mobile phones.

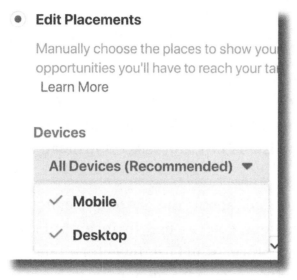

You can target your users based on the specific devices or operating systems they use. Your options are the following:

iOS Devices

- iPads
- iPhones
- iPods

Android Devices

- Android Smartphones
- Android Tablets

If you are running videos or ads to an area with slower internet speeds, and you want to ensure that your ads load quickly and without difficulty, target only users who are connected to Wi-Fi.

EXCLUDE CONTENT AND PUBLISHERS

Ads placed on the Audience Network, Instant Articles, or in-stream videos may appear alongside content that is not relevant or appropriate to your brand. For example, your ad may appear within a dating site or a controversial video. To protect your brand, you can exclude certain content or publishers with whom you do not want any association. The categories you can exclude are dating, debatable social issues, gambling, mature, and tragedy and conflict.

If you want to view the list of Facebook's publishing partners where your ads can potentially appear, go to Business Manager, click **Brand Safety,** then **Publishers List,** and select **Download Publishers List.**

Inventory Filter

If you are worried about the system placing your ads next to questionable content, you can use the inventory filter. You can choose among full inventory, standard inventory, and limited inventory. With full inventory, your ads will appear alongside the content of all of Facebook's publishing partners, giving you the widest reach. In contrast, with standard inventory, your ads will not appear alongside sensitive content. If you choose limited inventory, your ads will not appear alongside moderate and sensitive content, lowering your reach.

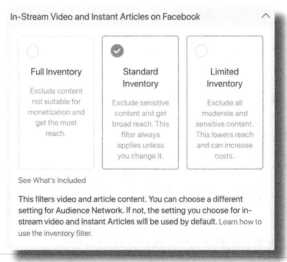

Audience Network Block Lists

If there is a specific website or app you do not want your ad to appear next to, you can also create block lists by uploading a spreadsheet of website domains and app store URLs that you want to block. Additionally, you can prevent your ads from appearing within the live streams of Facebook's gaming partners. If you want to remove specific domains, app store URLs, or Facebook page URLs, you can enter up to 10,000 items in a block list that you create.

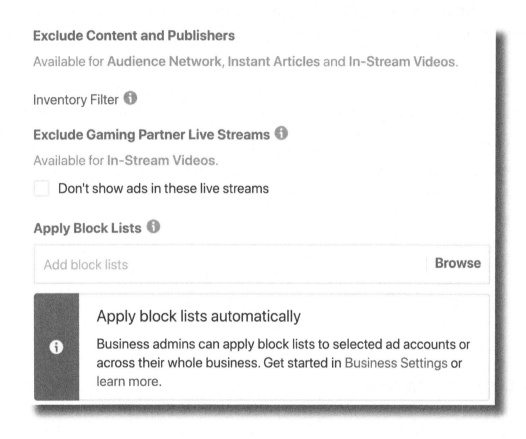

ADS

Creating your ads is the third and final step needed to launch your campaign. Uploading ads can be daunting because there are different creative assets, ad types, placements, and restrictions for each of these combinations. If you run into any issues, you will receive an alert letting you know where the conflict is coming from and how to resolve it.

Automatic Naming Template

As your ad account grows, it becomes important to name your ads correctly so you can quickly find specific ads and make adjustments.

As you would in the campaign and ad set levels, you can create a template for your ad's name by clicking the sprocket icon. You can use the following templated fields in your ad name:

- Ad Updated Date
- Current Ad ID
- Display Sequence
- Image Hash
- Page ID
- Identity

- Call to Action
- Current Ad Name
- Headline
- Instagram Account ID
- Custom Text

Every ad on Facebook's platform must be linked to a business page or Instagram account, which you can do in your Business Manager settings; otherwise, you cannot continue to the next steps. If you do not have an Instagram account or if you have not yet linked the account in Business Manager, you can run ads on Instagram instead. The ads you run will be represented by the Facebook page you selected when you created your Instagram business profile.

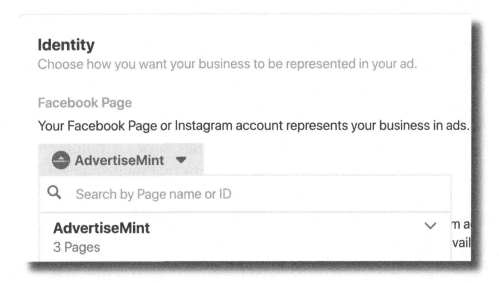

The profile image of your business page appears on the top-left corner of your ads. Once clicked, the profile image will direct users to your Facebook page. Users can also enter the name of your business page into the Ads Library to view all of your past and current ads.

AD FORMAT

When you set up your ad, you can either create a new ad or use an existing post. If you choose to create a new ad, you will be treated to several formatting options:

Single Image or Video Ads

These ads include one image, video, or slideshow containing multiple images. Image ads work best for promotions that incite quick decisions, for example, a flash sale. Video ads work best for capturing attention or telling a story, whether about your business, product, or services.

Carousel Ads

These ads contain 2 to 10 scrollable square images and videos. They often work well with telling a story, explaining the benefits of your business, and showcasing the features of your product. You can arrange images and videos in the order that you wish or arrange them in order of popularity.

Collection Ads

These ads allow you to attach multiple product images to the bottom of a video or image ad in News Feed. Once users click on the image or video, a product catalog will open with a button that redirects to the brand's website. Collection ads have three templates: instant storefront, instant lookbooks, and instant customer acquisition.

Instant Experience Ads

Formerly known as Canvas ads, the Instant Experience format allows you to build a custom full-screen mobile experience. Similar to a landing page built for mobile devices, this format can include clickable and scrollable images, videos, product feeds, text, and a variety of other elements. You can easily build the pages to appear exactly as you wish. Although this ad type takes a bit of time to create, no Facebook ad is as immersive and interactive as the Instant Experience ad.

AD CREATIVE

The media for your Facebook ads can be images, videos, or slideshows. Each has its own specifications with which you must abide.

Images

You can use new images, images used for previous ads, images uploaded to your Facebook or Instagram business pages, or royalty-free stock photos. Images can be horizontal (16:9 ratio), square (1:1 ratio), or vertical (4:5 ratio).

Facebook will slow or stop ad delivery if the image has more than 20% text. To test whether your ads violate the 20% text rule, use Facebook's overlay tool:

www.facebook.com/ads/tools/text_overlay

Videos

You can upload new videos, videos used for previous ads, or videos uploaded to your business page. Videos can be horizontal (16:9 ratio), square (1:1 ratio), or vertical (4:5 ratio). Stories ads, which appear only on Instagram, follows the 9:16 ratio. Certain placements will limit video length; for example, Instagram videos must be under 60 seconds.

Slideshow and Video Creation Kit

Video Creation Kit allows you to create stunning slideshows with images, text overlays, and logos. The Video Creation Kit comes with several templates designed for both square and vertical formats to help promote and sell products and drive product discovery. You can learn more about the Video Creation Kit online at Facebook's help center for businesses:

https://www.facebook.com/business/help/216283662383974

AD COPY

There are three areas in an ad where you can include your copy: the primary text, headline, and description. Because the copy will display differently for different ad formats, it is important to check each ad using the Ad Preview tool, which appears on the right side of your screen.

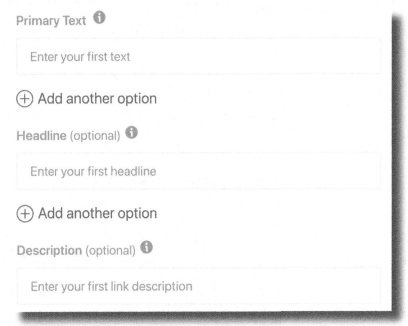

Primary Text

The primary text appears above Facebook ads, below Instagram ads, and below Stories ads as the call-to-action button. Although there is no maximum word limit, texts will be truncated after three lines. Users will need to "click view" more to read the remaining message.

The primary text should capture attention, compliment the ad's image or video, and communicate the heart of your marketing message. Many brands include emojis in their copy. If you choose to do so, make sure it is appropriate to your brand. Emojipedia is a helpful copy-and-paste resource you can use:

https://emojipedia.org/

Headline

The headline, the largest text in the ad, appears in bold. An optional field, the headline will appear next to the call-to-action button. Try to keep the headline between three and eight words, communicating your product's benefit to potential customers. While all Facebook and Instagram ads include headlines, Stories ads do not.

Description

Also optional, the description appears only on News Feed ads. On mobile News Feeds, the description will appear only if the headline is shorter than three to five words, contrary to desktop News Feed, where descriptions always appear. Although there is no limit on word count, descriptions are truncated after 33 characters. In your description, include information about your product or service that supports your headline.

When adding text for your ads, you will see a button "+ Add" on the bottom right of each text block. Clicking this button will add another text block. You can add up to five variants for each text block. When you save your ad, a new ad will be created with each variant you entered.

DESTINATION

The destination is the landing page where users will be redirected after clicking the call-to-action button on your ad. Your options depend on the objective you choose. For conversion campaigns, your destination can be a website or a Facebook event. For app installs, it must be the page where users can download your app. For lead ads, it will be the lead form you selected. Make sure to use the correct destination that matches the offer or message in your ad.

URLS

If you want to send users to a landing page or website, you must enter the URL in the website URL field. Although Facebook does not allow URLs that redirect, it does allow shortened URLs that lead to a fixed location. You can enter your shortened URL in the Display Link field. Using shortened URLs is recommended, as landing-page URLs are often long and overwhelming to users.

If you want to track your results and send critical UTM variables to Google Analytics, you can click the **Build a URL Parameter** link or use Google URL builder:

https://ga-dev-tools.appspot.com/campaign-url-builder/

If using the Google URL builder, you must enter UTM codes in the following fields. All UTM codes must be written in lowercase to match how other ad platforms send UTM data.

Website URL

> https://www.advertisemint.com   ☐ Preview URL

Build a URL Parameter

Display Link · Optional

> Enter the link you want to show on your ad

Campaign Source
This is the source of your traffic, which is often Facebook, Messenger, or Instagram. If you are targeting all placements, list the source as Facebook. If your code includes a space, replace the space with an underscore (_).

Campaign Medium

This is your advertising medium or placement. You can enter "all_placements," "newsfeed," or "stories."

Campaign Name

This is the name of your campaign. For Facebook ads, this is the objective. You can enter "clicks," "conversions, "app_installs," and "store_visits."

Campaign Term

This is the name of your ad targeting. For Facebook ads, it includes details about the users you are targeting or the segment of your ad funnel users are in.

Campaign Content

This is the name of your ad, and it should contain the ad format and promotional details. You can enter " videos" or "images" for ad type, "blackfriday," "sale," or "giveaway" for promotional details.

If you want to dynamically enter elements from your Facebook ads into your UTM fields, you can enter the following codes:

ad_id = {{ad.id}}

adset_id = {{adset.id}}

campaign_id = {{campaign.id}}

ad_name = {{ad.name}}

adset_name = {{adset.name}}

campaign_name = {{campaign.name}}

placement = {{placement}}

site_source_name = {{site.source.name}}

The final link should appear like this:

https://www.advertisemint.com/?utm_source=facebook&utm_medium={{placement}}&utm_campaign={{campaign.name}}&utm_content={{ad.name}}

If you have Google Analytics installed on your website, the data will appear under **Acquisition > All Traffic > Source/Medium**.

CALL TO ACTION

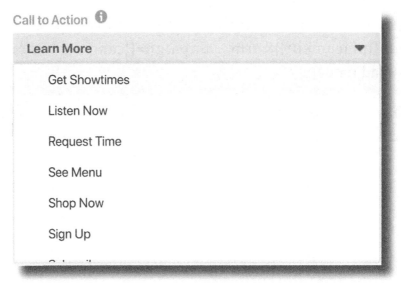

The call-to-action (CTA) button appears on the bottom-right corner of every Facebook ad and on the bottom-left corner for Instagram ads. These are pre-selected buttons that encourage users to take action. Different objectives will unlock different CTA buttons:

- Apply Now
- Contact Us
- Download
- Get Offer
- Learn More
- Play Game
- See Menu
- Sign Up
- Watch More

- Book Now
- Donate Now
- Get Quote
- Get Showtimes
- Listen Now
- Request Time
- Shop Now
- Subscribe

Because different CTA buttons will have different results for your ads, it is recommended that you test and determine the one that works best for your business.

STORIES CUSTOMIZATION

When you create your ads, Facebook will take your ad content and create a version that will appear in the Stories format for Instagram, Facebook, and Messenger. You can edit the background color of your ad to match the ad content.

Branded Content

If you are posting as part of a paid sponsorship, you must disclose the sponsorship by using the Branded Content feature. Facebook's ad policy requires a sponsored tag within posts by creators or publishers that are influenced by a business partner for an exchange of value.

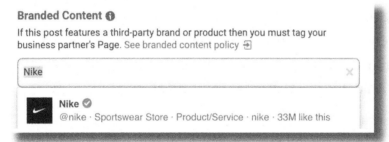

When you include a sponsored tag in your post, an extra line will appear above the post, containing the name of the brand with whom you have a paid partnership. Users can click on the sponsor's name to visit its business page.

Languages

If you wish to create a single campaign with ads in multiple languages, make sure you select an objective that supports multiple languages, such as traffic, app installs, conversion, video views, reach, and brand awareness. You must first select the primary language. Afterward, you can enter up to 48 additional languages. You can edit the ad copy specifically for the chosen language.

TRACKING

There are a few final details you must review to ensure your ads are tracking correctly.

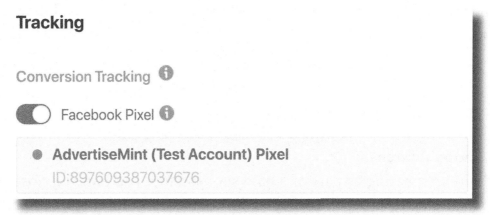

Facebook Pixel

Although the pixel is typically assigned to each ad, you must ensure that the pixel listed under the conversion tracking field is the same pixel you have on your website. You must also make sure the pixel is marked by a green dot, which indicates that it is firing correctly. If you launch a campaign without a working pixel, your campaign will experience issues with delivery, performance, and ad spend.

App Events

If your ad utilizes an app event, such as an app install or an in-app purchase, make sure the App Events box is checked and the correct app selected.

Offline Events

You can enter any offline events you want to track in the Offline Events field. Common examples are in-store purchases or orders made through phone calls. When you upload this data to Offline Events, the conversions will be counted after the data is matched. You can set up your Offline Events in the Offline Events tab of Business Manager.

AD ACCOUNT OVERVIEW

Your Ads Manager account overview gives a full view of your ad campaign's activity and data. There are specific tools in the overview that you should use:

Date Range
This feature filters account data according to the dates they were running. For example, you can view accounts that ran last month, last year, or last week. You can even find lifetime campaigns (campaigns that have been continuously running).

Performance
If you want to know how your campaigns are doing, you can click the columns tab and scroll to the Performance button. You can choose specific performances you want to view, such as delivery, engagement, video engagement, and app engagement, among many others.

Breakdown
This tab shows you the breakdowns of your campaigns. If you want a report of your audience's age in your campaigns, you can filter by age. If you want to see other data for gender, country, region, or impression device, among many others factors, you can also find that in the breakdown dropdown menu.

Reports
The ads reporting tool stores all of your saved reports. To save your reports, click on the reports tab. You can export reports as tables, share the link of the report, or create a custom report.

Ad Delivery
The delivery section shows your conversion locations, pixel events, optimization for ad delivery, the allocated conversion window, your bidding method, and charging method.

DISAPPROVED ADS

It is likely that one of your ads will be disapproved at least once. If that happens to you, you can take several actions. One, you can edit the ad to meet Facebook's ad policies. Two, you can contact your Facebook representative if you have been assigned to one. (Only accounts or agencies with large budgets can have a representative.) Three, you can appeal the disapproval using Facebook's appeals form:

Facebook Ad Appeals
https://www.facebook.com/help/contact/1582364792025146/

CHAPTER 4: FACEBOOK AD POLICY

To run Facebook ads, you must abide by the company's ad policies. The policies change frequently, and you can find the latest version online:

https://www.facebook.com/policies/ads

When you submit your ads to Facebook for review, both its AI machine and human employees will review each ad's image, video, text, ad targeting, and landing page to ensure they abide by the policies. If your ads are in compliance, they will be approved and will run within 24 hours. If your ads fail to meet one of Facebook's policies, they will not be approved, and you will receive an email stating the policy that was violated. You will need to edit the ads according to Facebook's disapproval details.

It is possible for your ads to be falsely disapproved. If this happens, you can appeal the decision by completing Facebook's appeals form:

Facebook Ad Appeals

https://www.facebook.com/help/contact/1582364792025146/

Multiple ad violations can lead to a disabled ad account. It will also tarnish the credibility of those managing the account in the eyes of Facebook, making it difficult to run Facebook ads in the future.

PROHIBITED PRODUCTS, SERVICES, AND PRACTICES

Facebook's ad policy lists the items you cannot advertise on Facebook. The list below is the condensed version of the original policy. To view the original, visit Facebook's Ads Policy page.

Facebook Ads Policy
www.facebook.com/policies/ads

1. Illegal products or services
2. Discriminatory practices
3. Tobacco and tobacco paraphernalia
4. Unsafe supplements
5. Weapons, weapons modification accessories, ammunition, and explosives
6. Adult products, services, and content
7. Third-party infringement
8. Sensational content
9. Targeting personal attributes
10. Misleading or false content
11. Controversial content
12. Non-functioning landing page
13. Surveillance equipment
14. Bad grammar and profanity
15. Nonexistent functionality
16. Implying or assuming personal health
17. Payday loans, paycheck advances, and bail bonds
18. Multi-level marketing
19. Penny auctions and bidding fee auctions
20. Counterfeit documents
21. Low-quality or disruptive content
22. Spyware or malware
23. Ads with automatic animation
24. Unauthorized streaming devices
25. Circumventing Facebook's systems
26. Deceptive or misleading financial products and services
27. Sale of body parts

RESTRICTED PRODUCTS AND SERVICES

Restricted products and services are allowed on Facebook under certain criteria. You can view more details regarding restricted products and services at **www.facebook.com/policies/ads**.

1. Alcohol: Ads targeting alcohol must target the correct drinking age for each country.

2. Dating: Ads promoting online dating services can be approved only with Facebook's written permission. Advertisers must apply to be a registered dating partner to qualify.

3. Real Money Gambling: Ads promoting real money gambling can be approved only with written permission and must target users who are 18 years old or older.

4. State Lotteries: Only lotteries run by the government are allowed.

5. Online Pharmacies: Ads for online and offline pharmacies are allowed with written permission.

6. Over-the-Counter Drugs: All ads promoting over-the-counter drugs must comply with all applicable local laws and guidelines, and must include age and country targeting to comply with local laws.

7. Subscription Services: Ads promoting subscription services must meet Facebook's subscription services requirements.

8. Financial and Insurance Services: Ads for financial services must provide full disclosure regarding fees. Ads for loan services must not ask for users' financial information.

9. Branded Content: Ads promoting branded content must tag the brand.

10. Political Advertising: Political ads must adhere to Facebook's authorization process and local laws as long as they comply with Community Standards and Advertising Policies.

11. Cryptocurrency Products and Services: Cryptocurrency ads are allowed only with Facebook's prior written permission.

12. Drug and Alcohol Addiction Treatment: Advertisers must be certified with LegitScript and receive prior approval from Facebook.

13. Weight Loss Products and Plans: Advertisers must target individuals 18 years or older and cannot include before-and-after images.

ADDITIONAL AD POLICIES

Facebook has additional ad policies on the following topics and may add more at any time. Learn more about these by visiting Facebook's ad policy.

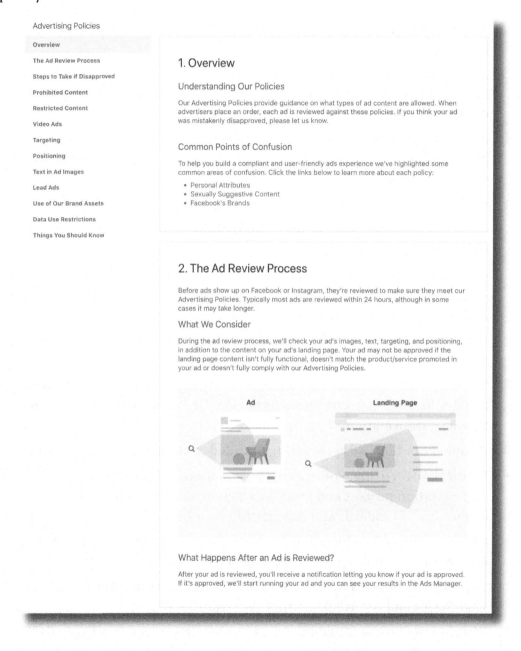

CHAPTER 5: SPECIALIZED AD TYPES

If you want to increase your customer list or promote your products from your catalog, you must learn about two ad formats: the Lead Ad and the Dynamic Product Ad.

LEAD ADS

With Lead Ads, you can collect valuable information from potential customers, such as phone numbers, email addresses, and job titles, without directing them outside Facebook's platform. The information these users provide will be stored in Facebook's servers, which you can download as a CSV form. To automatically funnel leads to your CRM, you can integrate two applications to your Lead Ads:

Zapier
Zapier is an automation tool that allows you to integrate your Lead Ads with your CRMs and create sequence to nurture your leads. When you connect Facebook to Zapier, the leads your ad acquired will automatically import to the CRM of your choice, such as MailChimp. This is especially helpful when you are scaling your ads. For example, rather than downloading 100 leads a day from Facebook, you can, instead, allow the integration to download those leads to your CRM. Once the leads are in your CRM, you can sequence those leads, for example, automating an email to send to one of your leads.

To connect Facebook with Zapier, visit the Email by Zapier website:

https://zapier.com/app-directory/email/integrations/facebook-lead-ads

Leads Bridge
Leads Bridge is similar to Zapier. When you connect your Lead Ads to Leads Bridge, your newly attained leads will automatically import to your CRM. Once they are downloaded, you can segment your leads and apply automation rules and filters.

To save 25% on Leads Bridge, use code ADVERTISEMINT25.
https://www.leadsbridge.com

DYNAMIC PRODUCT ADS

Dynamic Product Ads dynamically create different versions of themselves when users visit a product page, add products to their carts, or make purchases. Because Facebook's system can see the exact steps those users made and the product they saw, Dynamic Product Ads can create a specific ad featuring the product each user viewed. You have most likely seen this type of ad in action when you view a product, and suddenly that specific product appears all over the internet.

Dynamic Product Ads work exceptionally well for retargeting customers who interacted with your business, for example, people who added your products to cart without checking out. After you upload your product catalog, the ad will show relevant products to users. This ad type is especially beneficial for businesses in the e-commerce, travel, automobile, and real estate industries.

Dynamic Product Ads for Shopping

When users click on your ad to view a specific product from your catalog, Dynamic Product Ads automatically advertise the exact item users viewed. To run Dynamic Product Ads, you must have a Facebook Pixel or SDK, a Business Manager account, and a product catalog. If your website is supported by Shopify, Magento, or BigCommerce, you do not need to set up a product catalog in Business Manager.

Dynamic Product Ads for Travel

Dynamic Product Ads automatically retarget travelers who visited your website, showing them lodgings, flights, and destinations that they are most likely to be interested in. The ads will use information from your website, such as availability and pricing, then promote relevant products from your catalog. For example, if a user viewed your villa in Italy, the Dynamic Product Ad will retarget that same user with the same villa she viewed.

Dynamic Product Ads for Automotive

Dynamic Product Ads pull automobiles from your inventory and show them to users who are shopping for a new vehicle. For example, if users viewed your 2019 Ford Ranger, your Dynamic Product Ads will show that same vehicle to those users. The ad will contain important information about the product, such as make, model, and year.

Dynamic Product Ads for Real Estate

To run real estate Dynamic Product Ads, you must have a Facebook page, ad account, catalog, and pixel installed on your site. Like the travel and automobile ads, real estate ads pull products from your inventory and display them to interested users. The catalog in your ad must include home listing ID, name, images, address, neighborhood, latitude, longitude, price, availability, and listing URL.

Dynamic Product Ads work well because they act as reminders about the items people have viewed. Because these ads are often the most profitable ads you can run on Facebook, you should create them first if you own an e-commerce company. Facebook also values these ads more because they indicate a higher level of consumer intent.

Best Practices for Dynamic Product Ads

- Make sure your creatives make sense when combined.
- Make sure you have at most 30 creatives.
- Make sure you have at most five text variations.
- Have no more than 10 image or video variations.
- Have no more than five headline variations.
- Have no more than five link description variations.
- Have no more than five CTA-button variations.
- Create only one form for Lead Ads.
- Write generic copy that applies to all products.
- Keep your copy short.
- Do not add text to images.
- A/B test multiple CTA buttons to find the most effective one.

Instant Experience

An Instant Experience Ad takes you to an immersive, interactive experience. Once clicked, this ad type unfolds to full-screen view on your mobile phone. Once you are in the world of Instant Experience, you can swipe up, down, left, right, or zoom in and out to follow the ad's narrative. Each part of the ad's creative, whether it be an image or a video, can, if desired, include links to your landing page.

If you want to create an Instant Experience Ad, make sure to use one of the following objectives:

- Traffic
- Conversions
- App Installs
- Engagement
- Video Views
- Brand Awareness

There are two ways to create an Instant Experience Ad: using a template (the easier option) or using the Advanced Instant Experience Ad Builder (the harder option). To create this ad format, go to the ad set level and click Add an Instant Experience.

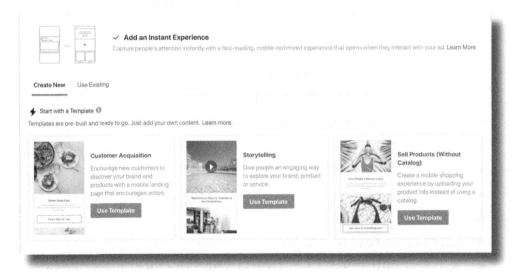

3D POSTS

Facebook allows you to upload a 3D image that you can click on and rotate to see a full 360 view of the featured object. Unfortunately, you cannot create 3D ads by uploading your files to Ads Manager or by boosting the 3D post. You can, instead, raise brand awareness among your current followers by organically sharing a 3D post from your Facebook page.

When creating your 3D image, keep these requirements in mind:

- File type: GLB file
- File size: 3MB or smaller
- Textures: jpeg and png
- Height and width: under 4,096 pixels
- Rendering methodology: PBR and KHR_materials_unlit extensions

Also, keep these tips in mind:

1. In the post copy, encourage users to click and drag on the image.

2. Feature products. 3D images work best for this.

3. Encourage users to examine your image by making the featured subject look realistic.

4. Design objects to appear in motion, which are more enticing to click and examine.

5. Because Facebook does not support 3D animation, make sure not to include that.

360 VIDEOS

Although you currently cannot upload 360 videos to Ads Manager to create an ad, you can, instead, upload it to your page's Timeline and boost the post. Otherwise, you will have to add the 360 metadata yourself before uploading the video. The video you upload must have been taken by a special camera, such as the Samsung Gear 360 or the ALLie Camera.

To upload a 360 video to your Timeline, follow these steps:

Step 1: Click the camera icon from your empty status update to upload video.

Step 2: Click **Advanced**.

Step 3: Click **This video was recorded in 3D format > 360 Controls > Publish.**

Step 4: Click Facebook's notification about your upload. **Click Edit Video Page > Save.**

Step 5: Click **Boost Post** once the post appears on your Timeline.

The 360 video will contain a 360 icon in the middle of the preview to distinguish itself from regular videos.

Keep these tips in mind when filming your video:

1.   Add traditional audio if you are targeting mobile and desktop devices.
2.   Add ambisonic audio if you are targeting VR devices.
3.   Keep a steady hold on your camera.
4.   Place your camera where you want to place your viewers.
5.   Craft a story that encourages users to explore your video.
6.   Place the camera at mid-chest height so people do not appear warped.

APP INSTALL ADS

Linking App to Accounts

App Install Ads allow you to advertise your apps to users. Once users click your ad, they will be redirected to the app store where they can install your app. To create App Install Ads, you must first connect your app to the Facebook for Developers website and to Business Manager. Only then can you use your app to create App Install Ads.

To link your app to your Facebook for Developers account, you must follow these steps:

Step 1: Download the Facebook SDK.

iOS: https://developers.facebook.com/docs/ios/

Android: https://developers.facebook.com/docs/android/

Step 2: In Business Manager, go to App Dashboard, click **Add a New App**. Create a new app ID. Select **Create App ID**.

Step 3: Complete security check.

Step 4: Add a product to integrate with your app and set up the product following the steps on your screen.

Step 6: Click **Settings > Advanced**. Set up your settings.

Step 7: From the menu, click **Roles** to assign roles. Enter the name or username of the person you would like to add. Only admins can create App Install Ads for your app.

Step 8: From the menu, click **App Review**. Slide the toggle bar to **Yes** to make the app public.

To link your app to Business Manager, follow the steps below:

Step 1: Go to Business Manager > Business Settings > Apps.

Step 2: Add your app using your app ID.

Step 3: Assign ad accounts to your app.

Step 4: Assign partners to your app.

Once you have connected your app to the SDK and to Business Manager, it will be available for attachment when creating App Install Ads.

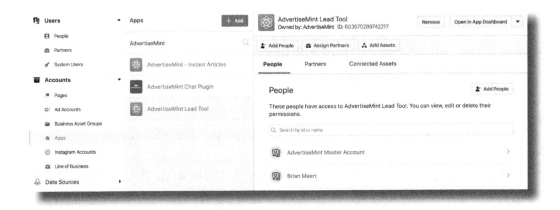

CREATING AN APP INSTALL AD

App installs is the only objective eligible for the App Install Ad. When you create the ad, you will be prompted to select mobile devices and operating systems. Because Facebook automatically chooses the devices and operating systems compatible with your app based on the type of app you have, you should not worry about this section unless you want to specify the device versions you want your ad to appear in or unless you want your ad to appear only in devices that are connected to Wi-Fi. During the ad-creation process, you will also be asked to provide your preferred optimization in the ad set level. You should optimize for the goal that you want to achieve, which, in this case, is app installs.

Choose your conversion window, bid amount, charges, ad schedule, and delivery type. Remember that your conversion window is the amount of time between someone clicking or viewing your ad and completing an action you have defined as a conversion event, such as purchases. If you choose a one-day conversion window, Facebook will track your customer's actions on your website for 24 hours, whether that action is viewing other products, adding to cart, or purchasing.

STORE TRAFFIC ADS

Setting Up Business Locations

You can use the Store Traffic Ad to advertise multiple business locations in a single ad unit. Once clicked, the ad will direct users to the location closest to them. To create a Store Traffic Ad, you must first set up the main page of your business location. A main page functions more like a branding page than a business page. While a business page contains your business address, reviews, and ratings, a branding page does not because it represents your business as a brand rather than a specific brick-and-mortar store. If you choose a business page to be your main page, the address, reviews, and ratings shown on the page will disappear. This happens because your business page will be converted to a brand page.

Step 1: From Business Manager, go to **Business Locations**.

Step 2: Click **Setup Main Page > Get Started**. Choose your page, then click **Make [page name] my main page**. Add your store locations.

If you cannot find your page from the dropdown menu, you can contact Facebook support and ask them to set up Business Locations for you. They will respond to you within 24 hours, and they will set up your business location's main page within two to three business days.

SETTING UP A STORE TRAFFIC AD

When creating the ad, you must select the business locations. You can add locations by entering your locations' ZIP codes, store numbers, or designated market areas (DMA). You will also be able to set your radius size, or the area around each of your business locations that you want to target users in. You have two choices for your radius size: audience and distance. If you choose audience, Facebook will target ads to the number of people you want to reach. If you choose distance, Facebook will target users within the radius that you choose.

In the ad level, you will need to choose your ad's voice, for which you have two options: main page and local pages. If you choose the main page, your ad will contain only your business's name. If you choose local pages, your ad will contain both your business name and its city location. You will also choose a page, a website URL, or a store locator destination. In the first option, the ad, once clicked, will send users to your business's Facebook page. In the second option, users will be redirected to your business's URL. In the third option, they will be directed to a map where they can find your business' location.

OFFERS ADS

The Offers Ad includes discount codes that customers can use at checkout or in store. If you want to create this ad, you must select one of the only two eligible objectives: conversion and traffic.

When creating an Offers Ad, you must turn on the offer feature and create your offer by including a title, the offer details, and the offer schedule (when it expires). You must also choose a redemption location and a promo code.

Redemption location: You can allow code redemption online or in store. If online, you must add the website URL where users can redeem your offer.

Promo code: You can exclude a promo code, add one code, or add unique codes. If you add one code, multiple users will be able to use the one code you created. If you add unique codes, each user will have different codes to use.

The final step, which is optional, is to implement advanced options. In this step you can prevent people from sharing your coupon, and you can upload the terms and conditions for your offer.

MESSENGER ADS

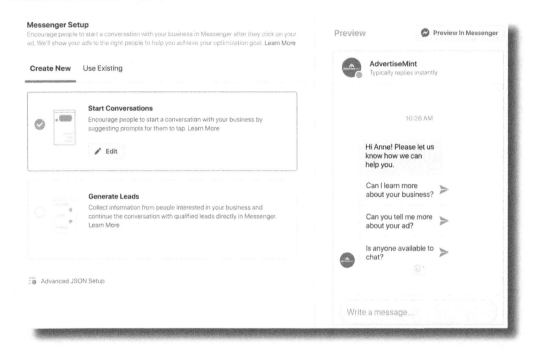

Messenger Ads send customers directly to your conversation window after they click on your ad. You can use this ad format to send customers discount codes, guides, or infographics. To create a Messenger Ad, you must choose either the traffic, conversions, app installs, reach, Messages, brand awareness, or catalog sales objective. You must also choose Messenger as the option that asks for your traffic source, or where users will be taken after clicking on your ad. At the ad level, you will set up Messenger to greet and respond to the users who are directed to your conversation window. There are two greeting templates: standard and custom.

STANDARD TEMPLATE

Enter your text greeting. The text greeting is the first message your customers will receive upon entering your Messenger conversation. Then personalize your message. You can either choose to personalize the message according to first name only, last name only, or full name. When you personalize your message, the name in the greeting will change according to the person contacting you.

Next, select a list of responses. The responses you choose must be relevant to your business goals. For example, if you want customers to learn more about your business, add a "Learn more" response. You can also choose a response that will answer commonly asked questions. For example, if people often ask about quotes for your services, add a "What are your agency rates?" response to the greeting.

Custom Template

Custom template goes beyond the text-only template. This option allows you to customize your greeting with photos and videos, add buttons that send customers to your website, and create quick, automatic replies so that you can respond to customers even when you are away from your computer or smartphone.

When creating buttons, you have to provide the label, action, and website URL. The label is your CTA button that encourages customers to take an action. The action options in the second field are "Open a website" and "Send a postback." Unless you have a chatbot, select the first option, "Open a website," then add the website URL where you want your customers to go after clicking your label. For example, you can add "View Rates," which, once clicked, will send customers to the pricing page of your website.

COLLECTION AD

Facebook launched an enhanced version of video ads that allow customers to find and buy the product featured in the video. This new format is called the Collection Ad. The Collection Ad allows you to attach multiple product images to the bottom of a video or image ad in News Feed. For example, if your video ad features the Pure Boost ZG Trainer Shoes, you can attach images of those shoes to the bottom of the ad. Once customers click on the image, they will be taken to a product catalog Facebook hosts. Note, however, that although customers can access the catalog through the platform, they cannot make a purchase from the app. Rather, once they click, they will be taken to your website where they can purchase your products.

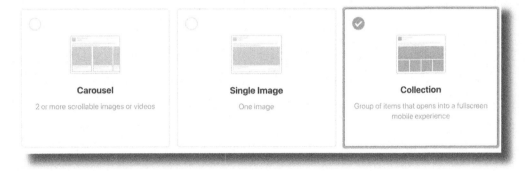

When creating a Collection Ad, you must choose among three templates:

Sell Products: Use this template if you want to feature your products. The ad will appear as a grid displaying the items you want to sell.

Showcase Your Business: Use this template if you want to showcase your business for your brand awareness campaign. The ad will be in a full-screen, interactive format that users can click and scroll through.

Get New Customers: Use this template if you want to drive people to your landing page. This ad will appear in an interactive, full-screen format. Users can scroll up and down to read more information and click on your CTA button, which will send them to the web page of your choosing.

In addition to choosing a template, you must also select the thumbnail for your ad. Use a thumbnail that provides a sneak peek of the ad's message, sparks intrigue, and compels your audience to click.

Next, you will add your product catalog. You have two options:

Order dynamically: With this option, your ad will automatically show people the product that is relevant to them. This is the recommended option.

Choose a specific order: With this option, the products from your catalog or the products you manually enter will appear in your ad. The products featured will not change according to your audience's interest or behavior.

SLIDESHOW ADS

The Slideshow Ad is a lightweight format that loads and plays easily in areas with low internet speeds and older cellphone models. It is composed of 3 to 10 still images. You can use images from video stills, a photo shoot, or photos from Facebook's free photo library. In addition to images, you can also include music. Slideshows can be as short as 5 seconds or as long as 50 seconds.

When creating a Slideshow Ad, you must add your media, text, links, and pixel at the ad set level. In the media section, you can add the media for your ad. Next, you need to write the copy. You must write copy for your text, headline, and link description. When writing your copy, make sure it is grammatically correct, relevant to your overall offer, and concise.

Once you have added your media and copy, you must include your website URL. This is the destination to which your ad will send your customers. For example, if you want customers to know about your business's services, You would add the URL that directly sends your customers to your services page. Always check that your website link matches your ad's description. For example, do not advertise your product catalog and, instead of providing the correct URL, add the link for your about page. Doing so will direct your customers to a page that they did not expect, causing them to feel deceived.

Next, you must choose your CTA button, display link, and pixel options. The CTA button you choose must describe the action you want your customers to take and must be relevant to your landing page. For example, if the website URL you provided will direct them to your product catalog, and you want your customers to purchase from that catalog, choose "Shop Now" or "Buy Now" as your CTA button. The display link, conversely, is the link that appears on the ad. Although this feature may not appear on all placements, placements such as Facebook

News Feed will show the display link to customers.

Finally, you must track conversions from your Facebook Pixel. Although optional, it is highly recommended that you do so. Before you submit your ad for Facebook's approval, always check that you enabled pixel tracking. As you are editing from the ad level, you will see a preview of your ad on the right side of your screen. You can click the dropdown menu above it to preview your ad in other placements. Once you are satisfied with your ad, you can click **Confirm** to submit your ad to Facebook. Once your ad is approved, you will receive an email notification.

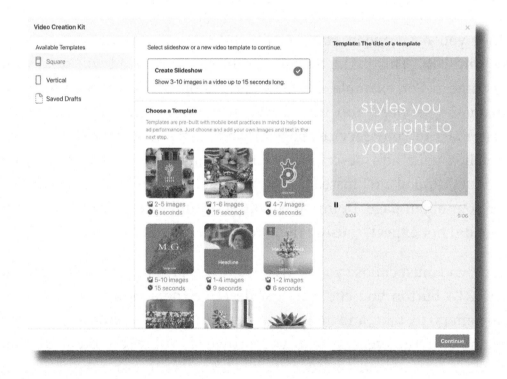

CHAPTER 6: HOW THE AD AUCTION WORKS

Facebook advertising is an auction in which you set a bid to win a spot in News Feed for users to see. You are competing against other advertisers whose target audience is similar to yours. To win the auction, your ad must have the highest total value, which is determined by your bid, your estimated action rates, and the ad quality.

https://www.facebook.com/business/help/430291176997542

BID

Your bid is the amount you are willing to pay for an ad's desired outcome. To bid in the ad auction, you must set your budget and your bidding strategy. You can bid with or without cost control. You have three cost control options: cost cap, bid cap, and target cost. Choose target cost if you want to pay for consistent costs, cost cap if you want to pay for the most volume, or bid cap if you want to control costs while reaching as many users as possible.

ESTIMATED ACTION RATES

Estimated action rates is the metric Facebook uses to measure the probability of whether or not a user will click on and convert from your ad. High estimated action rates will increase your ad's value and, consequently, the probability of your ad winning the auction. Although clickbait and engagement have been common practices among inexperienced advertisers, this method is banned and does not affect your ad's estimated action rates.

AD QUALITY

Facebook measures your ad's quality by evaluating reports from users. For example, if your ad has been reported in the past, that report will negatively affect your ad-quality score. Similarly, if customers have been giving your products low ratings on Facebook, thus impacting your customer feedback score, your ad will be considered as low quality in the eyes of Facebook's system. Violation of Facebook's ad policies, such as engagement bait, will also affect ad quality.

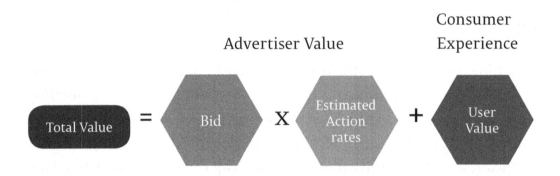

CHAPTER 7: BUSINESS MANAGER OVERVIEW

Facebook introduced Business Manager so that you can manage all of the aspects for your ad accounts beyond merely creating ads in Ads Manager. You can, for example, manage your Custom Audiences lists, reporting, and billing information.

BILLING

You can set up multiple payment settings, view invoices, and see charges on your account in the Billing page of Business Manager.

To add a payment setting, click the **Payment Settings** button. You can add a credit or debit card, Paypal, Facebook ad coupon, or bank account.

As you run ads, Facebook will bill you in small threshold amounts, usually $250 or $500. Each time your ad spend reaches this level, the billing method on file will be charged. If a payment method reaches its limit or has issues processing, Facebook will pause all of your ad campaigns until it is resolved. It is recommended to have two more billing methods on your account so that if one method has an issue, your ads will continue to run.

Each account has a safety feature called Account Spending Limit. Using this feature, you can choose the master amount you are willing to spend on Facebook ads. When this amount is activated, the ads will stop running when the amount is reached. You can change, remove, or reset your spending limit at any time.

If you are scaling your ads and expecting to spend more than $5,000 a day, you will need to ask Facebook's billing department to request an increase in your daily ad-spend limit. You can reach Facebook's billing department through email or live chat.

Contact Facebook's Billing Department:

www.facebook.com/business/help

BRAND SAFETY

In the Brand Safety tab in Ads Manager, you can manage your block and publisher lists and publisher delivery reports.

Block Lists

To create a block list, you will need to upload a TXT or CSV file that includes one URL per line that you wish to prevent from displaying your ads. The maximum line limit per file is 10,000. The type of URLs you can block include website domains, app-store URLs, and Facebook page URLs.

Publisher Lists

The publisher list contains all of the URLs where your ads could appear. The list, which contains thousands of links, can be downloaded or viewed. If you find a URL that you do not want associated with your brand, you can copy the link and paste it into your block list. Currently there are thousands of recorded publisher lists for the Audience Network, Instant Articles, and In-Stream Video:

Audience Network: 60,000 records

Instant Articles: 8,500 records

In-Stream Video: 65,000 records

Publisher Delivery Report

The publisher delivery report is a downloadable file that shows you all of the places where your ads have appeared in the past 30 days. Do not neglect this report. It is important to review because it shows you the exact sites where your ads are appearing and gives you the chance to determine whether those sites are inappropriate for your brand. The report is divided into three categories: Audience Network, Instant Articles, and In-Stream Video. The In-Stream Video and Instant Article reports will show the impressions you received on each publisher's site.

EVENTS MANAGER

The Events Manager page will show you an overview of all of your data sources, custom conversions, and partner integrations. It is also where you can add new data sources to your ad account.

To add a new data source, click the **+ Add New Data Source** button and select **Facebook Pixel, Offline Event Set** or **App Events**.

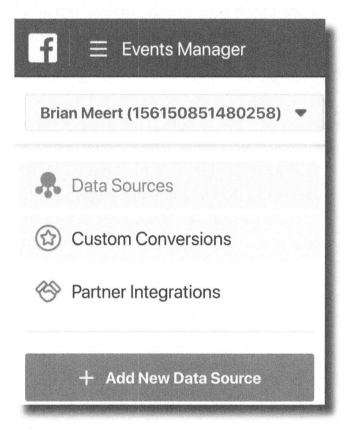

Facebook Pixel

By default, every ad account comes with a single pixel. Once you upgrade to Business Manager, you have the ability to create multiple pixels if needed. While it is not common, it is possible for one business to have multiple websites, for example, a pet store owner with one site for cats and another for dogs. In this case, instead of placing the same pixel on both sites, the owner should create a separate pixel for each site.

When adding a Facebook Pixel as a data source, enter the pixel name, paste the website URL, and press "Continue." Facebook will walk you through pixel installation, events testing, diagnostics, and settings. Once you have installed your pixel, you can use the pixel helper to verify that it is working correctly.

Custom Conversions

There are two ways to track conversion events with the Facebook Pixel. The first and most common is to use the pixel events tool, which fires on pages where customers take an action, such as viewing a product, adding items to cart, or completing a purchase. The second method is to use Custom Conversions.

Custom Conversions allow you to optimize and track for specific actions without adjusting your already existing pixel code, a process that requires replacing the pixels placed on the final page after the desired action is completed (e.g., order complete page). Although standard events are the preferred method of tracking because those fields appear first in the conversion tracking area, if you do not have a programmer on staff or if you are using an e-commerce platform such as Shopify, WooCommerce, or Magento, correctly implementing standard events can be a hassle, making Custom Conversions your best option.

Custom Conversions allow you to track a conversion event based on a URL string, which means you can enter the URL of the page you want to mark as a conversion, and Facebook will track all the users who make it to that page. You can apply rules to the URLs you choose. For example, you can apply a rule that instructs the pixel to record an event only when the event occurs on a URL page that contains certain keywords. You can combine rules to get even more specific.

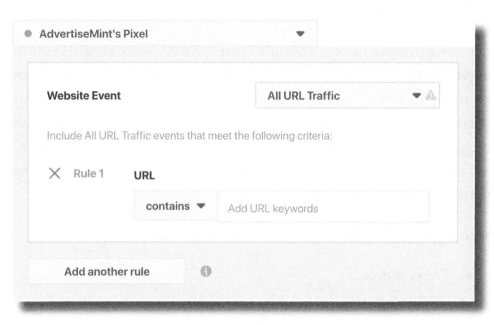

When creating a Custom Conversion, you will need to name your Custom Conversion, select a category, and enter a value (optional). Once this is completed, you will be able to view analytics for these Custom Conversions and monitor their progress over time.

PARTNER INTEGRATIONS

Installing pixels can be difficult if you are not familiar with coding. To help simplify this process, Facebook created customized walk-throughs for many of the most popular content management and e-commerce systems. You can view all of the partner integrations in the Partner Integrations tab under the Events Manager page. From there you can select any of the platforms you are using and follow Facebook's instructions.

Here is a list of the Facebook Partner Integrations:

- E-commerce
  - » BigCommerce
  - » 3dcart
  - » Ecwid
  - » Eventbrite
  - » Magento
  - » OpenCart
  - » PrestaShop
  - » Shopify
  - » Storeden
  - » Ticketmaster
  - » WooCommerce
- Website
  - » Bandzoogle
  - » Drupal
  - » Jimdo
  - » Joomla
  - » Kajabi

- » Segment
- » Shopline
- » Squarespace
- » Teespring
- » Webflow
- » Wix
- » WordPress
- Offline Conversions
  - » Segment
  - » Zapier
- CRM and Marketing Software
  - » HubSpot
  - » Infusionsoft
  - » Salesforce
  - » Zoho CRM
- Tag Management
  - » Google Tag Manager
- Mobile Platforms
  - » AppsFlyer
  - » Adjust
  - » mParticle
  - » Singular
  - » Branch
  - » Kochava

If you do not see a partner you use, you can request a new partner by clicking **Request a new partner** here located at the bottom of the page.

IMAGES AND VIDEOS

The Images and Videos tab houses all of the images and videos you uploaded for previous and currently running ads. These assets upload while you create your ads in Ads Manager. If you have a large number of images or videos that you want to upload all at once, you can do so in this page.

When uploading images or videos in the ad set level of Ads Manager, you will find cropping tools that allow you to resize your media into square or vertical formats. I recommend using these tools because square and vertical media, which fill in the screens of mobile devices, often outperform landscape formats.

Because Facebook prefers videos that live on its platform, you will see much better results promoting a video you uploaded to Facebook than to YouTube. When uploading a video for your ads, always abide by Facebook's ad specs:

- Recommend MP4 format, but support all video files

- Video file size up to 4GB

- Minimum length is 1 minute

- Maximum length is 240 minutes

- Recommend Stereo AAC Audio Compression with 128kpbs+

To view a complete sheet with all video sizes and layouts by placement, visit:

https://www.facebook.com/business/m/one-sheeters/video-requirements

To view more information on uploading 360 videos, visit:

https://facebook360.fb.com/?ref=fbb_ads_guide_video

Invoices

This page shows you all of the invoices for your ad accounts. Other than the account administrator, only the partner with the finance editor or finance analyst role can access this page. You can search for invoices based on invoice number, ad account ID, "bill to," or advertiser. You can also filter invoices by date or by paid or unpaid status.

Invoices are now available in Business Manager.

You're not currently eligible to view invoices. To view invoices, you need to be authorized to access them within Business Manager.

Please contact an admin and ask them to assign the Finance Analyst role to you by going to the People and Assets tab in Business Settings.

STORE LOCATIONS

If you own multiple retail stores, you can upload each location to make sure correct information appears on your business page or in search results on Facebook or Instagram. Uploading store location also allows you to run Store Traffic Ads. You can manage all of your retail locations by visiting the Store Locations page in Business Manager:

https://business.facebook.com/business_locations

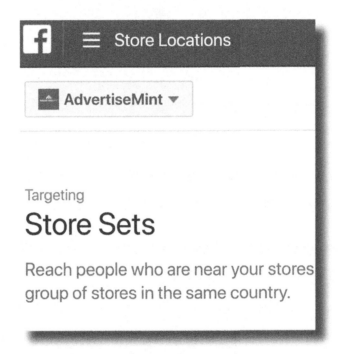

Home

The home page of Store Locations shows an overview of all of the stores you uploaded to Facebook's system. Facebook provides recommended actions if there are certain fields missing or incorrect information for each location. At the home page, you can also add new stores. Clicking the Add Stores button will take you to the Stores page.

STORES

The Stores page also contains an overview of all of your business locations. From this page you can edit, remove, or add new stores. You can also customize the columns used for reporting or segment reports by country, region, or city. To add a new store, select the Add Stores button.

At the home page, you can also add new stores by manually adding each address, uploading a file (for adding locations in bulk), or connecting an existing store page.

When manually adding a store, which is the ideal method for uploading fewer than 10 stores, Facebook will ask you for the business name, store ID, description, address, phone number, Wi-Fi network, subcategory, price range, store hours, and page username. Click "save" when finished filling the required information.

When adding multiple stores, you will need to upload a CSV file with the information for each location. This includes the same information you will provide for manually adding a store, but this method also allows you to specify whether the stores are part of a franchise and indicate the latitude and longitude coordinates of a specific location. Facebook provides a template for finding the latitude and longitude of your store once you upload your list.

Store Sets

Store sets are a group of stores in the same area. This feature allows you to reach people who are near your stores. After you select your stores, you can set the radius, for which you have three options: automatic radius with a maximum radius or a fixed radius. The radius can range between 1 and 50 miles.

BUSINESS SETTINGS

You can manage your ad accounts, pages, assets, Instagram accounts, data, and payments in the Business Settings page. If more than one person works on your social media or ad accounts, you can keep everything organized in Business Settings. Remember that the information you provide in your settings is visible to others working on your account.

Users

In this page you can add partners, assign assets to partners, and view the permission level for each partner. There are two types of users:

People are individuals to whom you want to give permission to certain account information. To add people to your account, click "add" and enter the email they use to log in to Facebook. Once done, a request will be automatically sent to them. When you select a person's name, you will see all the pages and ad accounts they have access to edit.

Partners are agencies or businesses that will be working on your account. Once you add partners, they, too, can provide access to multiple people in their organization to work on your account.

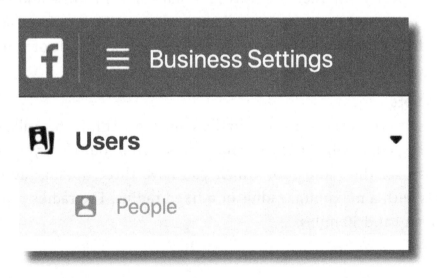

ACCOUNTS

The Accounts page in Business Settings contains information about your Facebook and Instagram pages, business asset groups, apps, and ad accounts.

Pages

From this page, you can add a page, request access to a page, or create a new page. If you have not yet added your existing page to Business Manager, you can do so by clicking "Add a Page" and entering the page name, which will appear in the suggestions dropdown menu. If you are the owner of the page, your request will be automatically approved. If you are not the page owner, you will need to choose the request access option and ask for admin permissions. Approved pages will appear as a list.

Below are the different kinds of access you can grant to a page:

Page admin can manage all aspects of the page. They can create ads, view insights, assign page roles, publish posts, and respond to comments and messages as the page, edit page details, and more.

Page editor can manage almost all aspects of the page. Like the admin, they can create ads, view insights, assign page roles, publish posts, and respond to comments and messages as the page, edit page details, and more.

Page moderator can create ads, view insights, assign page roles, publish posts, and respond to comments and messages as the page, edit page details, and more.

Page advertiser can create ads, view insights, manage branded content settings, and see which admin created a post or wrote a comment.

Page analyst can view insights, manage branded content settings, and see which admin created a post or wrote a comment.

AD ACCOUNTS

Every Facebook profile has an ad account by default, and you can view yours by searching for your ad account ID in the Ads Account page in Business Manager:

http://facebook.com/ads/manage

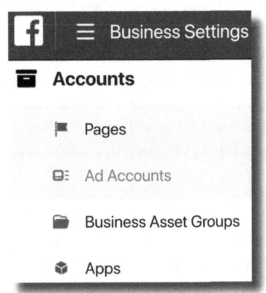

To add an ad account, select the **Add** button. You will have the option to add an ad account, request access to an ad account, or create a new ad account. To request access to add an ad account, you must provide the ad account ID, which can be found in Ads Manager or in the URL string of your ad account. Once an ad account is listed, you will be able to see anyone who has access to that account.

To create a new ad account, follow these steps:

Step 1: Click **Add > Create a New Ad Account**.

Step 2: Fill in required fields. Click **Create Ad Account**.

Step 3: Add people to your account and choose account roles.

BUSINESS ASSET GROUPS

Welcome to Facebook Business Asset Groups!

Business asset groups allow you to connect assets, people and permissions all in one place.

① **Add Assets**

Choose which Pages, ad accounts and pixels you want to group together.

② **Add People and Set Permissions**

Select who you want to be able to access the business asset group and grant permissions for each asset.

+ Create Business Asset Group

Business Asset Groups, which recently replaced the Projects feature, allows you to group multiple assets together and assign or revoke access to those assets. To set up a business asset group, do the following:

Step 1: Select the type of business asset to create. You have three options: separate brand, line of business, different regions, agency, or other. Afterward, name your asset group.

Step 2: Choose which assets you wish to assign to a group. You can choose to assign pages, ad accounts, pixels, Instagram accounts, offline event sets, catalogs, apps, and custom conversions.

Step 3: Select the individuals you want to add and the access level you want to provide to the individuals managing the assets.

APPS

If you want to run app install campaigns or target users based on app events, you must upload your app to Business Manager. To integrate your mobile app with Facebook, visit the Facebook Developers website:

https://developers.facebook.com/

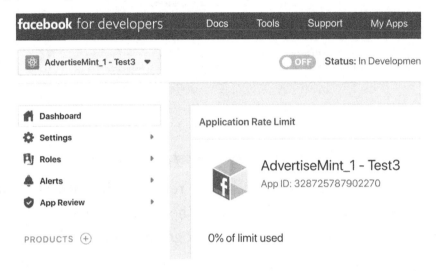

From there go to My Apps and click **Create App**. To link your mobile app to Facebook, you must install the Facebook SDK. You can view the SDK at the following Facebook for Developers page:

https://developers.facebook.com/docs/apis-and-sdks/

Once this is created, you can add the app to Business Manager by selecting **Add an App or Request Access to an App.** You will need the app ID, which you will find in the Facebook Developers website:

https://developers.facebook.com/apps/

Once an app is listed in Business Manager, you can provide access to people, partners, and connected assets.

INSTAGRAM ACCOUNTS

You can add Instagram accounts to Business Manager by clicking on the Add button. You must enter the username and password for the Instagram account you wish to link.

The Instagram account will appear, and you can view which people or partners have access. Once the login credentials have been validated, you will be able to select Instagram under the Identity section when you create your ads in Ads Manager.

DATA SOURCES

In the Data Sources page, you can view and manage your catalogs, pixels, and offline events sets.

Catalogs

Catalogs are files that contain product information advertised in Dynamic Product Ads. You can create new catalogs or request access to current catalogs in this page. You can create catalogs for products, hotels, flights, destinations, home listings, and vehicles.

To create a catalog, you must set permissions and then associate sources to the catalog, such as the Facebook pixel or a website, such as Squarespace. You must click "Add Items" to upload your products, which can be listed within a CSV or XML. If your inventory changes frequently, it is recommended that you set the file to automatically upload. You can set the upload schedule to hourly, daily, weekly, or whenever a new version is detected. You also have the option to upload the file manually. You can use Facebook's template file to ensure you correctly format the catalog.

To create a product catalog using the items listed in Shopify, WooCommerce, BigCommerce, or Magento, follow the step-by-step instructions provided by Facebook in its Help article:

https://www.facebook.com/business/help/1898524300466211

Offline Event Sets

Offline events are actions taken by customers outside of Facebook and online. The most common example is a person who purchases an item at a retail location after seeing that item on a Facebook ad. This conversion would be tracked only if you set up offline events to sync customer data back with Facebook. In the Offline Event Sets page, you can add or remove assets and assign partners and people to manage assets.

REGISTRATIONS

If you want your articles to be eligible for Instant Articles, a tool that allows your written content to quickly load within the Facebook app, you must register your news pages to Facebook. You can do this under the Registrations page of Business Settings. Once your request is approved, you can share information and assets, such as logos and editorial policies. You can learn more about news page registrations at the Facebook Business website:

https://www.facebook.com/help/publisher/316333835842972

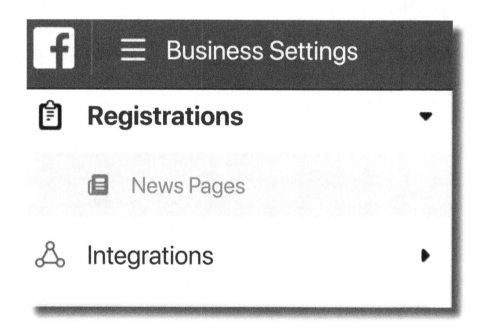

INTEGRATIONS

By default, any admins and connected CRMs will have access to your data collected by your Lead Ads. If you wish to customize the access to your leads, you can do so under the Leads Access page of Business Settings.

Payments

You can manage the credit cards on file or lines of credit that Facebook has extended to you in the Payments page of Business Settings. There you can also choose which businesses you wish to apply for credit.

Security Center

In the Security Center page, you can set up two-factor authentication for Business Manager, manage the roles of your admins and employees, and also add a backup admin in case you are locked out of your account. You can also apply for business verification.

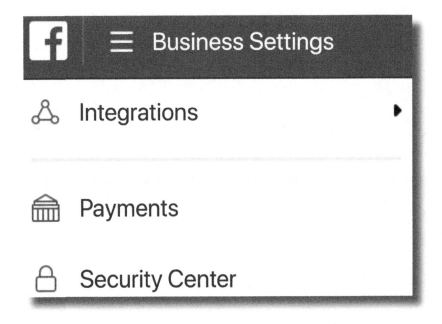

REQUESTS

The Requests page shows any pending requests to your Business Manager account. It will display requests received, requests sent, and invitations. You can confirm or decline the requests.

Notifications

In the Notification Settings page, you can select which type of business updates you wish to receive. These can include updates about business permissions, business roles, business updates, support, marketing updates, and partner program updates. You can configure the email that will receive these notifications for pages, ad accounts, WhatsApp accounts, catalogs, pixels, and apps.

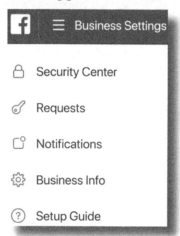

Business Info

Your business information will contain all the elements relating to your Business Manager account. It includes legal name, address, phone, website, tax ID, and contact name and email. You can update this information at any time.

Setup Guide

The Setup Guide will help provide tips, strategies, and walk-throughs for getting started on Business Manager. If you find Business Manager confusing, you should visit this page to get a better understanding of the tasks you need to do and how to complete them.

ADVERTISE

Ad Account Settings

The Ad Accounts page shows you the business information associated with your ad account. Here you can edit information such as ad account name, time zone, currency, advertising purpose, tax ID, and business address. It is important that you include the correct information for each field. For example, if you chose the wrong time zone, your ads will not run on the dates and times that you intended. Similarly, if you chose the wrong currency, you could spend more than you wanted.

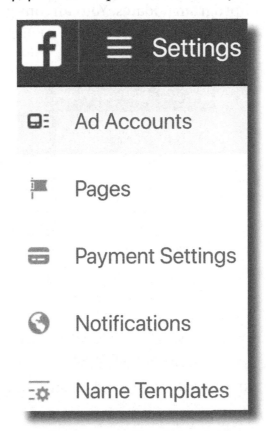

In the page, you can edit your attribution window, applying the new rule to all of your ads within your ad account, rather than doing so individually in Ads Manager. You can also edit ad account roles and partner permissions.

ADS MANAGER

Three Levels of Ads Manager

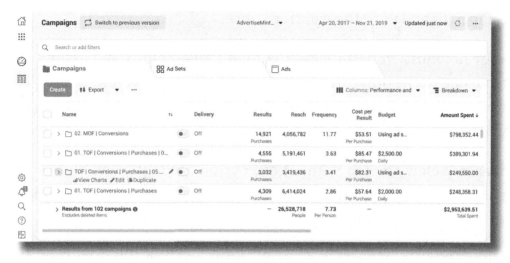

As mentioned in the previous chapters, Ads Manager is the dashboard where you create your ads. Ads Manager contains three levels: the campaign level, the ad sets level, and the ads level.

Campaign Level: In the campaign level, you can choose your objective and your special ad category (if applicable), create a campaign name, and enable split testing and campaign budget optimization.

Ad Sets Level: In the ad sets level, which contains one or more ads, you can choose your audience, schedule, budget, and placements, create separate ad sets for each audience, and choose either a daily budget or a lifetime budget.

Ads Level: In the ads level, which contains only a single ad, you can add creatives, copy, and links.

It is important that you understand these levels to easily improve your ad's performance. Understanding the structure helps you measure results, test different audiences, and identify which ads work best.

ADS MANAGER FEATURES

In Ads Manager there are helpful tools you can use to easily find your campaigns and view their performance.

Your Accounts: You can view all of your ad accounts and easily switch from one to the other. You will also find your ad account number here, which you will need when requesting ad account help from Facebook or when working with a partner who needs access to your accounts.

Search: Below the tab with all of your ad accounts, you will find the search tab, which you will use to search a campaign name, ad set name, ad name, and campaign ID, among many other factors.

Filter Options: Next to the search button is the filters button. With this, you can filter what you want to see on your ads report by delivery, objective, metrics, and more.

Filter by Days: You can also choose which campaigns you want to view by days.

View Your Performance: You can view performance related to delivery, engagement, video engagement, and app engagement, among many others aspects of performance.

Breakdown: Next to the performance tab, you will see a breakdown tab, which shows you the breakdowns of your campaigns, according to gender, country, region, or impression device, among many other factors.

Export Data: If you want to download the data for the campaign specifics you searched for, you can do so by exporting the files into a spreadsheet.

CREATING CUSTOM AND LOOKALIKE AUDIENCES

In this section, you will learn how to create Custom Audiences, Lookalike Audiences, and Value Based Lookalikes.

Custom Audiences

As mentioned in previous chapters, a Custom Audience is an ad-targeting tool that allows you to serve ads to your existing contact list acquired from Lead Ads, or to an audience tracked by the Facebook Pixel. You can create a Custom Audience in the Audiences page of Business Manager:

Step 1: Click **Create Audience** then **Custom Audience**. Choose your sources.

Step 2: Fill in the required information. Each source will ask for different files or information.

Step 3: Create audience.

If the source of your audience is a customer list, you must upload a TXT or CSV file that is correctly formatted for Facebook. You can download Facebook's Custom Audience template from the Ads Help Center in the Facebook Business website:

https://www.facebook.com/business/help/170456843145568

LOOKALIKE AUDIENCES

Lookalike Audience allows you to reach individuals who are similar to the people in your audience source. You can create Lookalike Audiences in the Audiences section of Business Manager, the same page from which you created your Custom Audience. To create a Lookalike Audience, you must follow several steps:

Step 1: Select Lookalike source.

Step 2: Select an event value.

Step 3: Select audience location.

Step 4: Select an audience size.

When creating a Lookalike Audience, you also have the option to use a source with an LTV, or lifetime value. By creating a Value-Based Lookalike, you are reaching customers who have spent the most on your business throughout the years. To create an LTV Lookalike, click "Create New Source" then click "Custom Audience With LTV." If you already have an LTV Custom Audience saved, you can use that by clicking on the empty field under Select Your Lookalike Source and clicking the file under Value-Based Sources.

AUTOMATED RULES

Successful Facebook ad campaigns require constant attention. There are many moving parts to your ad campaigns, and failure to monitor or manage your ads will result in higher advertising costs. Facebook created the Automated Rules feature to help automate tasks related to your campaign performance. For example, it allows you to automatically increase bids or ad spend if performance is good or lower bids and ad spend if performance is bad.

When you create an automated rule, you must choose an action (or the rule you want to apply when one or several conditions have been met) and a condition (or the circumstances in which Facebook must apply the rule you chose).

Apply Rule To: Where you want the rule to apply. You can apply a rule to all active campaigns, ad sets, or ads.

Action: What will happen when a condition has been met. Your options include turn off, send notification, adjust the budget, or adjust the manual bid.

Condition: This triggers the automated rule. You can choose from numerous conditions, but these are the most commonly used:

- Daily spend

- Lifetime spend

- Frequency

- Results

- Cost per result

- Mobile app install

- Cost per app install

- Mobile app purchase ROAS

- Website purchase ROAS

- Daily ratio spent

- Lifetime ratio spent

- Audience reached

After selecting a condition, set the thresholds to greater than, is equal to, is lesser than, or is not between, and enter a value and a time range. You can select the attribution window you wish to follow and then schedule the automated rule to run every 30 minutes, daily, or on a custom schedule.

When a campaign, ad set, or ad reaches the threshold in the time range you select, the automated rule will complete the action you chose.

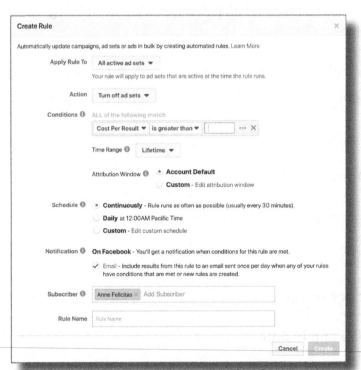

Here are a few examples of popular automated rules:

1. Turn off ads when frequency gets above a certain number.

2. Increase ad budget when cost per result is lower than the target cost.

3. Decrease ad budget when cost per result is higher than the target cost.

4. Increase bid if CTR is above a certain percentage.

5. Turn off ads after they reach a certain percentage of audience.

Make sure to give your rule a name. Note that you can toggle rules on or off at any time by visiting the Automated Rules page in Business Manager:

https://business.facebook.com/ads/manager/rules/management

You can review any action the rules have taken by visiting the Activity tab in the Automated Rules page.

CAMPAIGN PLANNER

Campaign Planner is a feature available to advertisers who have used the reach and frequency buying tool. It estimates the reach and frequency for a campaign based on the budget, ad placements, and target audience you choose. After you create a plan for your campaigns, you can compare one campaign with another and share campaign predictions with colleagues. To access this tool, go to the home page of Business Manager, click "All Tools" and then "Campaign Planner." This tool is a more advanced feature reserved for larger advertisers reaching a specific audience on a consistent basis.

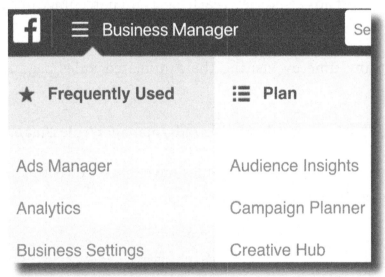

The results are broken down by frequency per person, placement distribution, and spend per day. To share the results, click the share button on the upper-right side of the screen. You can buy the plan by clicking Reserve for Purchase on the upper-right corner. The plan you create will automatically be saved. You can leave the screen and return to the plan at any time. If you wait too long to update your plan, it may become irrelevant. The status of your plan is represented in three different symbols: green circle, gray circle, and red triangle. Green circle means it is up to date; gray circle means it is not up to date; and red triangle means there is an error.

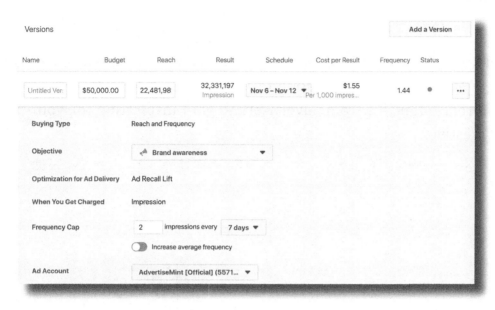

If you want to learn how to use the Campaign Planner tool, visit Facebook's tutorial in the Ads Help Center:

https://www.facebook.com/business/help/1776354522643452

CREATIVE HUB

The Creative Hub is a newly launched page in Business Manager that contains tools that allow you to create mockups, verify text image, and view available formats, among other activities. You can also look at different templates from advertisers to gain inspiration for your own ad creatives.

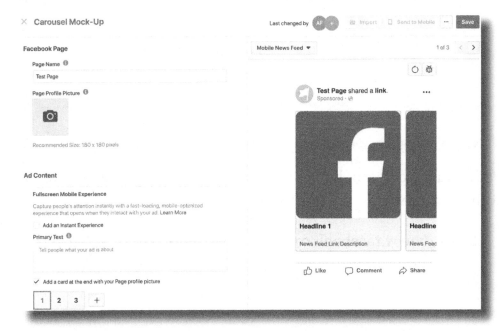

In Creative Hub, you can build creative mockups for the following ad formats:

- Facebook
  - » Carousel
  - » Collection
  - » Slideshow
  - » 360 Video
  - » Instant Experience
  - » Single Video
  - » Single Image

- Instagram
  - » Stories
  - » Stories Carousel
  - » Carousel
  - » Single Video
  - » Single Image

There is a page in Creative Hub called View Formats, which allows you to select a format and see what it looks like on certain placements. You can, for example, view what a Single Video Ad looks like in mobile News Feed, Instagram feed, and Instagram Stories.

Another page in Creative Hub is called Get Inspired, a gallery that contains samples of ads by some of the world's most popular brands in different formats, including Stories, Collection, and Instant Experience. Visit this page to receive inspiration for your next Facebook advertisement.

Remember, Facebook rewards ads that consumers find interesting. Spending a little extra time and resources in producing amazing creatives is a sure-fire way to increase the results from your ads.

MEASURE AND REPORT

If you want to view the data on your campaigns and analyze their results, you can do so within several pages of Business Manager.

Ads Reporting

The Ads Reporting page is perhaps one of the most under-utilized resources for Facebook advertising. Although Ads Manager provides data for core metrics as you edit your ads, if you want to see a more comprehensive analysis on your ad campaigns, you should visit the Ads Reporting page.

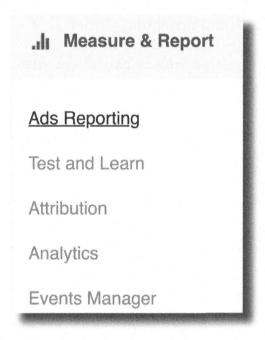

The Ads Reporting page will contain the reports of all of your ad campaigns. Because the number of files in this page will increase the longer you run Facebook ads, it may be hard to fish out the report you want to find. For this reason, the page contains filtering tools that allow you to find a report based on a specific criteria. For example, you can break down a report by ad level, time, and action.

Here are the different options for breaking down your report:

- Level

  - » Campaign Name
  - » Ad Set Name
  - » Ad Name
  - » Campaign ID
  - » Ad Set ID
  - » Ad ID

- Time

  - » Date
  - » Week
  - » Month

- Delivery

  - » Age
  - » Gender
  - » Business Locations
  - » Country
  - » Region
  - » DMA Region
  - » Impression Device
  - » Platform
  - » Placement
  - » Device Platform
  - » Product ID
  - » Time of Day (Ad Account)
  - » Time of Day (Viewers)

- Action

  » Conversion Device

  » Post Reaction Type

  » Destination

  » Video View Type

  » Video Sound

  » Carousel Card

  » Instant Experience Component

- Settings

  » Objective

- Dynamic Creative Asset

  » Call to Action

  » Description

  » Headline

- Image

- Text

- Video

- Website URL

In Ads Reporting, you can also compare attribution windows and create, export, save, or share a report. Remember that only individuals with access to the ad account will be able to view the report via a shared link.

ANALYTICS

In the Analytics page in Business Manager, you can view omni-channel analytics by selecting and grouping your event source groups, applications, pages, and pixels for your business. You access an overview of all of your reports, view insights, or create dashboards with information you want to track. Here is a quick walk-through of the important features found within this page.

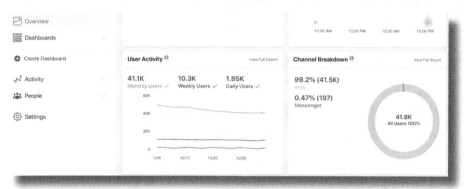

Overview

This area provides an overview of the most important reports, including:

- Growth Metrics
- User Activity
- Active Users by Hour
- Median Time Spent per User
- User Retention
- Lifetime Value for Paying Users
- Revenue
- Purchase by Device Type
- Repeat Purchases
- Gender
- Age
- Location

DASHBOARDS

Here you can create your own dashboard to analyze multiple data points.

Your dashboard options include:

- **Bar:** Compare quantities of users, events, or average purchase values.

- **Breakdown:** Analyze multiple categories of information at the same time.

- **Cohort Heat Map:** Measure retention or lifetime value by seeing how groups of people behave over time.

- **Cohort Trend:** Analyze a sequence of actions to measure conversion, drop-off, or completion time.

- **Funnel:** Analyze a sequence of actions to measure conversion, drop-off or completion time.

- **KPI:** Track and compare acquisition, retention, or other key metrics.

- **Overlap**: See how many people interact with your business in more than one day.

- **Pie**: Visualize proportions of users, events, or revenue.

- **Trend:** Track changes in user activity, events, or value over time.

There are also a few additional reports available to you:

- Activity

- Funnels

- Retention

- Cohorts

- Breakdowns

- Journeys

- Percentiles

- Events

- Overlap

- Lifetime Value

- People

- Demographics

- Technology

- User Properties

By using these reports, you will better understand how to reach customers more efficiently. As a rule of thumb, for every hour you spend building and targeting your ads, you should spend 5 to 10 minutes analyzing reports. Doing this will help you find the clues to improving your ad performance.

If you wish to view your analytics on the go, use the Facebook Analytics mobile app, available on both Android and iOS.

Google Play:
https://play.google.com/store/apps/details?id=com.facebook.analytics

App Store:
https://apps.apple.com/us/app/facebook/id1266461465

ATTRIBUTION

One of the most common questions business owners ask is, "How much money did this ad produce?" Ads are linked with desired outcomes, and the most common outcome is generating revenue. Today's consumers, who are tech-savvy, often switch between devices before completing an action, for example, clicking on a Facebook ad using a smartphone then purchasing from the website using a desktop device. This behavior poses a problem: Most clients use last-touch attribution, or the last ad clicked before an action, as the method to track their results. The last-click approach is the easiest to use, but it does not give an accurate representation of the ads that assisted customers during their purchase journey.

For example, if you are looking for a new car, you would begin to pay more attention to car commercials on TV. Then you might research car models on Google, review the features on the company website, and compare prices between new and used models on a car app. Only then will you head to a dealer, take a test drive, and purchase the car. If the business owner was using last-touch attribution, the dealership would receive all of the credit for the sale. The reality is different. It takes multiple steps (called multi-touch) to complete the sale.

Attribution answers the question, "Who gets credit?" It sounds like a simple issue to solve, but to get a full and accurate view of the story, it would require that Google, Facebook, Amazon, and all of the largest tech companies share their data with one another. There are a few companies trying to create data-sharing among the three digital advertising giants. Until a single perfect solution exists, the next best thing is Facebook's attribution tool, which provides key data about a customer's purchase journey. Although this tool is not perfect, it will help you better understand the actions your customers are taking within and off Facebook before completing a desired action.

To set up your attribution, you must select a line of business or create a new one, then select the event you wish to measure. You must then select a reporting period so Facebook can display all the events that occurred during that period. Last, you must select your attribution window. You can view performance metrics for paid traffic, organic traffic, and direct traffic. You can also create custom reports and view the conversion paths customers are taking before they complete an action.

There are three settings when building your attribution. The first includes selecting an attribution model:

- **Even Credit:** Gives an equal percentage of the credit for a conversion to each touchpoint on a conversion path.

- **First Click or Visit:** Gives 100% of the credit for a conversion to the first click or visit that happened on a conversion path.

- **First Touch:** Gives 100% of the credit for a conversion to the first click or visit that happened in a conversion path. If there was no click or visit, then it will credit the first impression.

- **Last Click or Visit:** Gives 100% of the credit to the last click or visit that happened in a conversion path.

- **Last Touch:** Gives 100% of the credit for a conversion to the last click or visit that happened in a conversion path. If there was no click or visit, then it will credit the last impression.

- **Positional 30% or 40%:** Gives a specific percentage of the credit for a conversion to the first and last touchpoints in a conversion path, with the remaining credit distributed evenly across all other touchpoints.

- **Time Decay 1-Day or 7-Day:** Gives an increasing percentage of the credit for a conversion to touchpoints as they get closer in time to the conversion.

The second involves selecting an attribution window:

- 1-day click and visit, 1-day impression

- 7-day click and visit, 1-day impression

- 7-day click and visit, 7-day impression

- 14-day click and visit, 1-day impression

- 28-day click and visit, 1-day impression (default choice)

- 28-day click and visit, 7-day impression

- 28-day click and visit, 14-day impression

- 28-day click and visit, 28-day impression

- 90-day click and visit, 30-day impression

The third choice is selecting your rules for credit:

- **Credits all visits:** Credits all visits normally.

- **Do not credit direct visits (default choice):** Credits paid and organic touchpoints. If there are no touchpoints before a conversion, then the conversion will be attributed to direct visits.

- **Don't credit any visits:** Credits clicks and impressions. If there are no clicks or impressions before a conversion, then the conversion will be attributed to direct visits.

If all this attribution talk seems confusing, you are not alone. Remember that Facebook's data defaults to using a 28-day click or 1-day view attribution method. Switching or adjusting these windows can help you get a better understanding of the actions driving your desired results.

AUDIENCE INSIGHTS

The Audience Insights page shows you a glimpse into some of the data Facebook has on its users. This information can help you learn more about your targeted customers or even your competitors' customers.

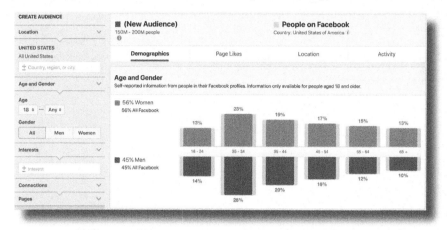

Facebook will display a variety of key data about the audience you selected using the criteria you chose in the left column. The information you can retrieve includes the following:

- Age and Gender
- Relationship Status
- Education Level
- Job Title
- Page Likes
- Location
- Frequency of Activities
- Device Users

The Audience Insights tool will display a gray bar to represent all users on Facebook and a blue bar to represent the audience you selected. You can use the data in Audience Insights to improve your ad targeting and ensure optimal results. It will be worth your time to do some research on your audience, which can help you improve your ad targeting and results. It will also most likely lower the amount you pay to reach your audience.

APP DASHBOARD

The app dashboard contains all of the apps you are advertising. From there you can view your app ID and app status. You can also add products to your apps and add new apps.

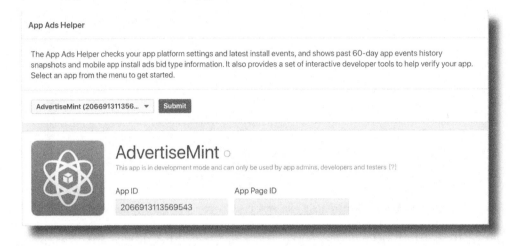

TEST AND LEARN

With the Test and Learn feature, you can run strategic tests that help you understand what actions work best for your business.

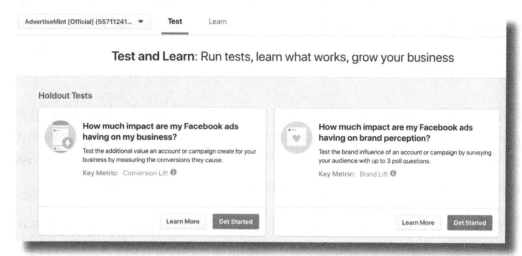

Facebook will provide several options for tests that are designed to help you measure improvements in conversion lift, brand lift, cost per conversion lift, and cost per result. When you select a test, you will be provided with information about the test: the way it works, the way it will be set up and the criteria for selecting the winning ad. Once you select your details, Facebook will run a test. When the test is completed, the details will appear under the Learn tab.

This feature is meant to help you run tests that show exactly which actions, creation, or bidding works best for your business. You can access the Test and Learn page in Business Manager:

https://www.facebook.com/test-and-learn/test

ENGAGE CUSTOMERS

Creator Studio

Creator Studio is a feature built exclusively for content creators or individuals who want to monetize their content. In Creator Studio, you can submit a post, go live, or upload content instead of using your business page, in addition to other capabilities. There are six tabs within Creator Studio:

Content Library: In this tab you can view all your posts, scheduled posts, drafts, and expired posts. It is an easy-to-navigate history of all the content you have posted. You can also see the videos you can cross-post or create playlists where videos display in a certain order.

Insights: Here you can view updates on the performance of your content, the loyalty of your audience, the demographics of your audience, and the earnings from your content.

Monetization: In this tab, you can check updates on your monetization, or the money you make from your content. You can also view collaboration metrics, apply for ad breaks, and create fan subscriptions.

Rights Manager: Here you can see whether someone is infringing on your copyright by illegally using your videos.

Sound Collection: This page contains royalty-free music to use in your videos.

Pages: This contains all of the pages you manage or access.

You can visit the Creator Studio by visiting:

https://business.facebook.com/creatorstudio

PAGE POSTS

The Page Posts section contains all of the page posts you have published on your Facebook page. From there you can see all of your scheduled posts, published posts, and ad posts, as well as metrics for all of your published posts, such as reach, engagement, and lifetime value. You can also create and delete posts from this section.

Published posts are posts you created using your business page. You can view the post title, post ID, privacy setting, reach, engagement, lifetime engagement, and date created in this page.

Scheduled posts are any posts you scheduled to publish at a future date and time.

Ads posts are any ads you created. When Facebook first created its ads platform, it allowed advertisers to run only Boosted Posts. As the platform grew, Facebook kept the original post ID as a way to represent each ad.

Post ID has one benefit: If you want to retain your social proof (likes, comments, and shares), you can use the post ID to create new ads in other campaigns and ad sets instead of duplicating the ad, which will not retain accrued social proof. This allows you to focus all of your advertising dollars toward a single ad that has been performing well, which will appear much more valuable to Facebook's algorithm.

SELL PRODUCTS AND SERVICES

In the Sell Products and Service section, you can access pages that allow you to view and manage all of the assets used to sell inventory on Facebook.

Catalog Manager

In the Catalog Manager page, you can build and manage the product catalogs for your Dynamic Product Ads. You can also use catalogs for the Instagram Shopping feature or for your Facebook Page shop.

There are four types of catalogs you can create:
- E-commerce (most common)
- Travel
- Real Estate
- Auto

If you use an e-commerce platform, such as Shopify, BigCommerce, 3dcart, Magento, OpenCart, Storeden, or WooCommerce, you can use Facebook's feature called Connect E-Commerce Platform, which will give you instructions on how to connect each platform, and its product catalogs, to Facebook. By using this feature, you are skipping the step of creating a catalog list and uploading the file to Business Manager.

If you do not use one of the aforementioned e-commerce platforms, you will need to click Update Product Info, give your catalog a name, select the pixel for that account, and click Create Catalog. Once your catalog is created, you will need to configure your event data sources and upload your product data to the catalog before you can run Dynamic Product Ads. The process of creating a product catalog is as follows:

Step 1: Go the Catalogs in Business Manager, click Create a Catalog, and select a catalog type.

Step 2: Select a catalog owner and catalog name.

Step 3: View catalog, upload file, and click Use Data Feeds.

Step 4: Choose Upload Once and then upload catalog.

EVENT DATA SOURCES

In order to run Dynamic Product Ads, your pixel will need to fire three events: view content, add to cart, and purchase. By firing during these events, Facebook can track users through the purchase process and show ads only to users who have not purchased. The Event Data Sources tab will show you if each of these events and the pixel are firing correctly.

Product Data Sources
Select **Add Products**. You will receive three options for creating your catalog:

Add Manually: For this method, you can add products one by one by uploading an image, name, description, content ID, website URL, price, and currency.

Use Data Feeds (Recommended): This method allows you to upload a CSV template of your product catalog or set up a file to update automatically as your product inventory changes. Download Facebook's template file if you are doing a one-time upload. If you want your catalog to upload automatically on an hourly, daily, or weekly basis, you will need to enter the feed URL.

Connect Facebook Pixels Using Microdata: This method requires you to implement microdata for products into your pixel. Microdata is additional pieces of information beyond just the name, price, and image. You can learn more about this method on Facebook Business:

https://www.facebook.com/business/help/1175004275966513

You can access your catalogs in the Catalog Manager page:

https://www.facebook.com/products

COMMERCE MANAGER

Using Commerce Manager, you can sell your products across Facebook and Instagram to users who can purchase your items without leaving the apps. Facebook has partnered with Shopify, BigCommerce, ChannelAdvisor, CommerceHub, ShipStation, Quipt, and Zentail to make this integration possible.

To set up Commerce Manager, you must link your business accounts, set your preferences, enter your customer service email, and link a bank account and routing number for your payouts.

To sell on Instagram, you will need to request approval and add your Instagram account to Business Manager. Once these steps are completed, you will be able to showcase your inventory in Marketplace and enable Instagram Shopping.

To learn more about Commerce Manager, visit Facebook Business:

https://www.facebook.com/business/help/2371372636254534

MONETIZE TRAFFIC

Monetization Manager

If you are a website or app owner who wants to generate ad revenue through the Audience Network, you can set up your website or app on Monetization Manager to view critical data about your traffic and earnings.

Monetization Manager helps you track and manage your monetization on the Audience Network. From there you can manage your ads and placements, analyze your ad performance, and optimize your revenue.

If you want to sign up for Monetization Manager, visit the Audience Network page:

facebook.com/audiencenetwork/products/tools/monetization-manager

Brand Collabs Manager

The Brand Collabs Manager helps you find public figures or influencers with whom you can have paid partnerships to help promote your brand. On this page, you can set your desired audience and search for influencers that are perfect for your brand. You can find influencers and their past work, their current audience, and their previous partnerships with other brands. You can also view reports about the status of each one.

To apply as a creator or to join as an advertiser, visit the Brands Collab Manager page:

https://business.facebook.com/collabsmanager/start/

CHAPTER 8: FACEBOOK ADS PRO TIPS

THE STOCKPILE METHOD

Facebook's advertising system favors ads that are valuable to users. One way Facebook determines the value of an ad is by looking at your engagement numbers (likes, reactions, comments, and shares). The more engagement you have, the more value your ad has to users. For this reason, having engagement on your ads contributes to their success in the auction.

Unfortunately, each time you duplicate or edit an ad, Facebook wipes away your engagement, hurting your ad's performance and results. You can retain your engagement by using the stockpile method. This method increases the lifespan of your ad because more of your budget will be focused into a single ad, signaling to Facebook's algorithm that the ad is valuable to users.

Step 1: Fill the required fields in the campaign, ad set, and ad level.

Step 2: In the ad level, click the **Ad Preview** button and select **See Post - Facebook with Comments**.

Step 3: Copy the post ID, which is the last 15-digit number that appears on the ad URL. If the URL is this, **facebook.com/245592755909602/posts/705549293247277**, then the post ID is **705549293247277**.

Step 3: Create a new ad using the post ID. This method will copy over the original ad and keep all of your engagement.

There are some things to note about this method. Once you create a new ad using the post ID, you can no longer duplicate the original ad. You can only duplicate ads using the post ID. If you edit the main ad, all of your engagement will be wiped away. Make sure all ad copy, creatives, links, and UTM tracking are in place before you save your ad.

SPLIT TESTING

If you are running ads for more than $10,000 a month, you should run split tests, experiments that help you find the ad that produces desired results. Running a split test presents several benefits. It may even be necessary in maintaining the performance of your ads.

If you are new to Facebook advertising, you might, instead of running a split test, edit your active ads. Doing this is a mistake because changes to the ad will reset the learning phase and remove ad engagement (likes, comments, and shares), another form of social proof. You should do everything in your power to avoid resetting your social proof, as the algorithm will stop the momentum of your ads, making it very difficult or impossible to get it started again. It is like a snowball rolling down a hill, growing larger and larger—you do not want to stop its progress. When you split test, you do not change your already active ads. Rather, you experiment prior to launching your ads on a full scale.

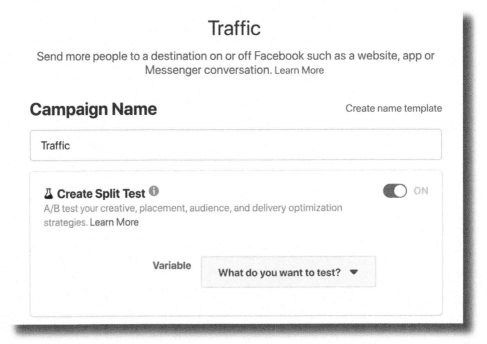

With split tests, you will notice no issues with ad delivery. This occurs because Facebook values split testing and prioritizes the completion of your test. During the progress, Facebook will provide valuable insights that will help you produce successful ads in the future.

A common argument is to run dynamic creatives and analyze the results rather than run a split test. Although an option, this method is not a statistically sound experiment. When you run a split test, the system will divide an audience in half, showing one group one ad version and the second group another. In contrast, if you use the method for dynamic creatives, the system will show ads to everyone, with the possibility for individuals to see multiple ads, invalidating the experiment.

COMMON SPLIT TESTS TO RUN

1. Ad Text

The text above an image ad or video ad is critical. You may be tempted to immediately push salesy messages, such as "Buy this now," but it is important to remember that you are talking to users with low purchase intent, users who are on the platform to socialize, not buy. Before you decide on the text that will appear on your ad, show your ad creatives to four or five colleagues and ask them to write the caption you think best suits the creatives. Run these ads as a test. You will be amazed to discover the version that performs the best.

2. Instagram vs Facebook

Many clients ask which platform performs better: Instagram or Facebook. Although you can see the results in the ad breakdown, it is still worth testing. Run a split test comparing Instagram and Facebook, using the same ad spend and ad creatives for both.

3. Video Length

Facebook recommends shorter videos, but when it comes to generating results, you might be surprised to find the video length that works best for your business. For your experiment, create a three-to-five-minute video highlighting your business and the value it brings to your customers. Then create shorter versions of the ad: 60 seconds, 30 seconds, 15 seconds, and 10 seconds. Run those against each other and see which one performs the best.

4. Bidding Strategies

With numerous elements involved, bidding can be confusing. For your test, run an ad with cost cap against an ad with bid cap.

5. Video Thumbnail

Often overlooked, video thumbnails are the still previews that people see before a video plays. The thumbnail can either entice people to watch the video or scroll right past. Test different clips for your thumbnail, featuring different important scenes from the video that you believe may attract users' eyes. An attention-grabbing thumbnail has been known to increase watch rates by more than 40%.

BUDGET AND SCHEDULE

Facebook does not charge you a fixed monthly fee for its ads because the ad buying process is a bid. Rather than charging you a set amount per month, Facebook will charge you from the budget you set. Your budget is the amount of money you are willing to pay during the lifetime of your ad. If, for example, you have a $20 daily budget, you will spend a maximum of $20 each day. Although you have $20 to spend each day, Facebook may not spend that entire budget. For example, Facebook may charge you $15 for the day, depending on your ad's performance in the auction. Although the charge per day may differ, Facebook will never charge you more than your daily budget.

When setting a budget, you have the option to choose between a daily budget and a lifetime budget. Your daily budget is the amount you will spend each day, and your lifetime budget is the amount you will spend during the duration of your ad set. You cannot choose your budget type while the ad is running. You can, however, duplicate an ad set and create a different budget type for that ad set.

For ad schedule, your default option is to run your ad set continuously. If you select that option, Facebook will run your ads until your budget has been completely spent. Your second option is to set a start and end date. Facebook will run your ad based on the start date that you choose and end it on the given end date. The times entered must comply with the times of each ad's location. Thus, if you start your ads targeted in New York and London at 5:00 p.m., both ads will begin at 5:00 p.m. in their respective locations.

When choosing your budget and your bid, it is recommended that you do not spend too low, as your ad will need to compete in the auction. Remember, Facebook considers the bid you place when ranking your ad's quality. The higher the score, the more successful your ad.

WHEN YOU GET CHARGED

You have three options for how you want Facebook to charge you. You can choose to be charged every time 1,000 impressions occur, every time someone clicks on your ad (CPC), or every time someone watches a certain percentage of your video (thruplay). If you choose per 1,000 impressions, Facebook will charge you every time your ad appears on your audience's screen.

If you choose link clicks, Facebook will charge you every time someone clicks on any part of your ad. This includes clicking to react, to comment, to share, or to claim your offer. If you choose thruplay, Facebook will charge you every time someone watches your video ad. If you are unsure which method would be more financially beneficial to you, you can test two similar ad sets with different charging methods.

Not all objectives are eligible for the same charging method. For example, while the video views objective is the only one eligible for thruplay, the rest of the objectives are eligible for either impression or link click. The chart below shows you the charging methods for each objective.

Objective	When You Get Charged
Brand awareness	Impression
Reach	Impression
Traffic	Impression, link click
Engagement	Impression
App installs	Impression, link click
Video views	Impression, thruplay
Lead generation	Impression
Messages	Impression
Conversions	Impression
Catalog sales	Impression
Store traffic	Impression

CBO (CAMPAIGN BUDGET OPTIMIZATION)

As mentioned in the Ads Manager chapter, Campaign Budget Optimization, or CBO, is a feature that ensures the system spends your budget optimally. Keeping your budget and bidding strategy in mind, CBO will allocate your budget toward your ad sets in a way that will get you the desired results. When enabling CBO in the campaign level of Ads Manager, keep these recommendations in mind:

1. **Be Patient.**
   It make take some time to see satisfactory results after you enable CBO because the system takes several days to learn. You will find that ad sets without CBO perform better than ad sets with CBO when they first run. However, after the system learns, the ad sets with CBO will perform better than the ad sets without CBO. Therefore, do not jump to conclusions during the first few days after enabling CBO.

2. **Do Not Use Ad Set Spend Limits.**
   Imposing too much budget limitation on your ad sets will make it difficult for Facebook's delivery system to optimize your budget. If you can, do not apply any spending limits. If you feel safer imposing limits, do so sparingly.

3. **Limit Ad Sets.**
   Facebook allows a maximum number of 70 ad sets with CBO campaigns. It is recommended that you use large audiences and only have two to four ad sets under CBO

4. **Make Sure Your Ad Is Delivering.**
   If an ad with CBO enabled is experiencing some delivery issues, Facebook's system will be unable to distribute your budget and deliver results. If your ad is not delivering, increase either your bid cap or your target cost. You should also change your targeting and ad creatives.

OPTIMIZATION OPTIONS

When choosing your optimization and bidding strategy, think of your goal. If, for example, you have an app installs ad with an app installs objective, choosing the app installs ad delivery optimization will show your ads to users most likely to install your app. If you wanted to pay only for every time users have clicked on your ad to download your app, the link click (CPC) bidding strategy will best complement your objective and delivery optimization. If you choose the right ad delivery optimization and bidding strategy, you will be closer to achieving your business goal.

Brand awareness: Facebook will serve your ads to an audience most likely to pay attention to your ads.
Link click: Facebook will deliver your ad to an audience that is most likely to click on your link at the lowest cost.
Impressions: Facebook will place your ad in front of your audience as frequently as possible.
Reach: Facebook will deliver your ad to your audience once a day.
Landing page views: Facebook will deliver your ads to users who will most likely click on your ad's landing page link.
Daily unique reach: Facebook will deliver your ads to users once a day.
Post engagement: Facebook will deliver your ads to users who will most likely like, share, or comment on your ad.
App installs: Facebook will deliver your ad to users who will most likely download your app.
App events: Facebook will deliver your ad to users who will most likely take a specific action on your app at least once.

Video views: Facebook will deliver your ads to users who will most likely watch your videos.
Leads: Facebook will deliver your ads to users who will most likely give you their contact information.
Replies: Facebook will deliver your ad to users who will most likely have a Messenger conversation with you.
Conversions: Facebook will deliver your ad to users who will most likely convert on your website.
Conversion events: Facebook will deliver your ad to users who will most likely take action when they see your product catalog.
Store visits: Facebook will deliver your ad to users who will most likely visit your business location.

DELIVERY

Facebook will deliver your ad to your target audience using two methods: standard delivery or accelerated delivery. If you choose standard delivery, Facebook will deliver your ads evenly over the course of your campaign (this process is also called pacing). Keep in mind that because Facebook paces your budget, Facebook may lower your bid when there are more inexpensive opportunities available to get the best results out of your budget. Pacing is advantageous to you because you will have the funds to spend on more inexpensive opportunities that may come later.

Delivery Type ⓘ
- **Standard (Recommended)**
  Get results throughout your selected schedule
- **Accelerated**
  Spend your budget and get results as quickly as possible

If you choose accelerated delivery, Facebook will deliver your ads as quickly as possible. The focus will be on speed rather than efficiency. Although this option may prevent you from getting the most cost-effective delivery options, it will be beneficial to you if your campaign is time-sensitive.

Sometimes you may find that your ad is not delivering. That is likely caused by the low total value of your ad, calculated by four factors: your bid, your ad quality and relevance, and your estimated action rates. The following is a checklist of what you can do to increase your highest total value:

1. Do not bid low: Although you can bid any amount you want, it is important not to bid too low. If a competitor bids a higher amount for a spot in News Feed that you want, you will lose the bid and the spot.

2. Create high-quality ads: Low-quality ads may affect delivery.

3. Target a relevant audience: If you target the wrong audience, you will receive a low relevance score, which will result in low estimated action rates, or the number of people Facebook predicts will respond to your ad.

It is important for your ad to have a high total value; otherwise, your ad will not deliver.

DYNAMIC PRODUCT AD OPTIMIZATION

In the Budget and Schedule section of the ad set level, you will need to choose how you want Facebook to optimize your ad for delivery. If you do not choose carefully, Facebook will not deliver your ads, and your ads will fail. You have three options to choose from: link clicks, impressions, and conversion events. If you choose link clicks, Facebook will show your ads to those who will most likely click on your ad. If you choose impressions, Facebook will show your ads to as many people as possible. If you choose conversion events, Facebook will deliver your ads to those who are most likely to take action when they see a product from your catalog.

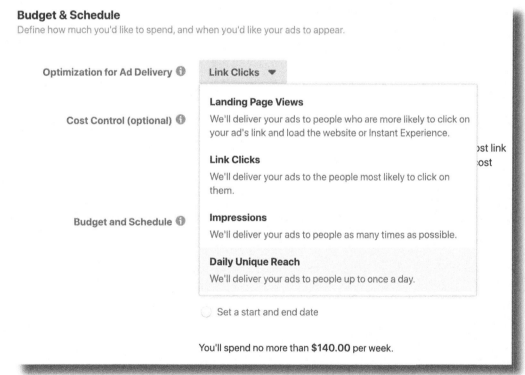

The two popular options are impressions and conversion events. Your choice between these two options depends on the amount of website traffic. If you have a small product catalog and little website traffic, then you should choose impressions. If you have a plethora of products and website traffic, then you should choose conversion events. It is necessary that you have a robust amount of website traffic when choosing conversion events because Facebook requires at least 25 conversions a week to gather enough data for optimization. If you do not have enough conversions for the conversion events optimization, Facebook will not have enough data to know to whom to show your ad, and your ad will not deliver.

You can choose to define your conversion event as an add to cart, a purchase, a complete registration, an initial checkout, or a search. If you defined your conversion event as a purchase, Facebook will optimize your ad by delivering it to those who will most likely make a purchase.

DYNAMIC PRODUCT AD FORMATS

For Dynamic Product Ads, you can choose the Carousel Ad or the Single Image Ad format. When you choose the Carousel Ad format, your ad will feature up to 10 images of products that your customers viewed, placed in their carts, or purchased. It will also feature products that are closely related to products your customers bought. When you choose a Single Image Ad format, your ad will feature only one product that your customers either viewed or added to their carts.

When deciding which of these two ad formats to use, ask yourself this question:

Do I want to encourage my customers to buy more products, or do I want them to buy only the product they have previously viewed or added to their carts?

If you want the former, then use the Carousel Ad format. If the latter is the case, then use the Single Image Ad format. Although both are valuable, use the Carousel Ad because it encourages customers to scroll through the carousel cards, consequently increasing the ad's relevance score. Additionally, the Carousel Ad format for Dynamic Product Ads is usually inexpensive compared to the Single Image Ad format.

BROAD DYNAMIC PRODUCT AD

Dynamic Product Ads work exceptionally well for retargeting customers who interacted with your business, for example, people who added your products to cart without checking out. However, Dynamic Product Ads prevent advertisers from acquiring new customers. If you want to retarget and acquire new customers, you can instead use the Broad Dynamic Product Ad, which targets a broad audience, people who expressed interest in your products or products similar to yours without visiting your website or app. After you upload your product catalog, the ad will show relevant products to users. To run a Broad Dynamic Product Ad, you must turn on your Facebook Pixel and upload your product catalog.

To create a Broad Dynamic Product Ad, you must go to the ad set level, go to the Audience section and click **Create New > Define a Broad Audience and Let Facebook Optimize Who Sees Your Products**.

Although not required, you can refine your audience and exclude certain groups. From the Audience section, click Show Advanced Options.

- No exclusions: You do not exclude anyone from seeing your ads. Even people who already purchased from you will see your ads.

- Exclude people who purchased: The ad will not appear to people who already purchased your products.

- Create a custom exclusion: Your ads will not appear to people based on the rules you specify. For example, you can choose to exclude people who purchased a specific brand of shoes in the last 10 days.

It is recommended that you exclude people who already purchased, as they are unlikely to convert again. However, you should include all website visitors. There are also two additional best practices to keep in mind for this ad type:

1. Do not use Lookalike Audiences, behavioral targeting, and interest targeting, as they will limit your ad's delivery.

2. Optimize for conversions.

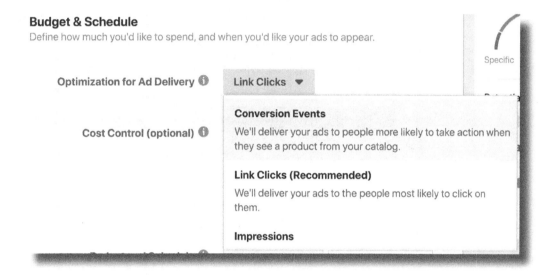

DAY PARTING

Day Parting, which you can enable by switching your ad set's spend to a lifetime spend, allows you to run ads at specific days or at specific hours. Advanced advertisers use Day Parting to create relevant, time-sensitive ads and ensure their target audience never sees the same ad twice.

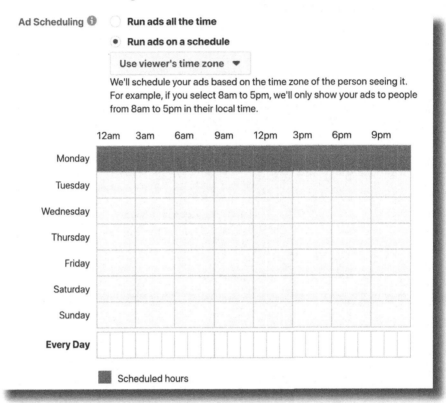

Here is one example of how you could use Day Parting: Set up an ad set that targets website visitors from the last seven days. Set the ad set's budget to a lifetime budget, select day parting, and highlight all the time slots on Monday. Create an ad that references Monday, such as a Cyber Monday sale. Create an ad set for each day of the week, each with a unique ad that references its corresponding day of the week. Once the ad runs, visitors who come to your website will immediately see a series of seven ads over the next week regardless of the day they visit your website. Test new ads that correspond to each day to improve results.

TARGETING EXPANSION

Targeting Expansion is a feature located in the ad set level of Ads Manager, underneath the Detailed Targeting box. With this feature enabled, your ad will reach a broader group of people than the audience you defined in Detailed Targeting, or people whom Facebook predicts will complete your objectives.

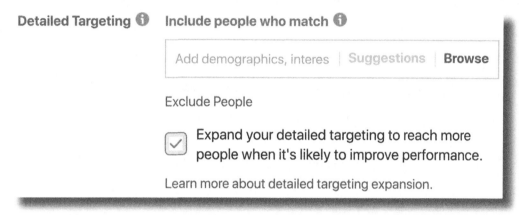

For example, if you are targeting New Yorkers, then serving them ads promoting an event in New York and selecting Targeting Expansion may also cause your ads to appear to individuals in New Jersey, given that Facebook predicts those individuals to be likely to respond to your ads. Although this tool may sound foolproof in theory, there is a downside. Revisiting the previous example again, Facebook could also show your ads to individuals in Alaska or Hawaii who are interested in an event similar to the one you are promoting. If you want to enable Targeting Expansion, you must monitor your campaign's performance very closely. Be careful when using this tool. It may seem beneficial, but it is like giving your child a credit card and sending them to a toy store. Do not be shocked when you see the bill.

SHARING AND EDITING PIXELS

To edit the title of your pixel, follow the steps below:

Step 1: Go to the Pixels page of Business Manager then click on the pixel you want to edit.

Step 2: From the upper menu, click the pencil icon next to your pixel.

To share your pixel, follow these steps:

Step 1: From the Pixels page of Business Manager, click on your pixel, then click Share from the upper-right corner of the top menu.

Step 2: In the field under People, enter the name of the user with whom you want to share your pixel.

OFFLINE EVENTS

Offline Events is a tool that allows you to track offline conversions. For example, if a customer clicked on your Facebook ad, deliberated for a few days, and visited your nearest brick-and-mortar store to buy your product off the shelf, Offline Events will track the data and show you that your ad influenced the customer's offline action. To track offline conversions, you need to create an Offline Events set where you can upload your data.

Step 1: Go to Offline Events, then click Add New Data Source > Offline Event Set. Fill in the fields, then click Create.

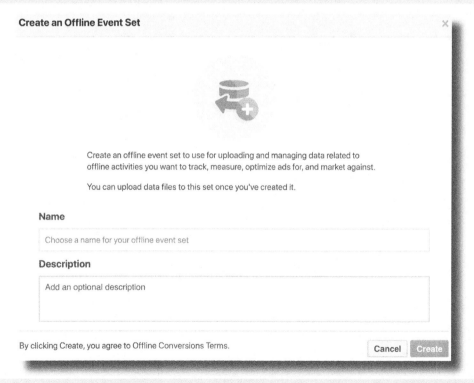

Step 2: Assign ad accounts and people to test the Offline Events set (optional).

Step 3: Upload and review file.

FACEBOOK PIXEL HELPER

The Facebook Pixel Helper is a Chrome extension that troubleshoots errors and improves performance. You can download the Pixel Helper for free from Google Chrome's web store. Once downloaded, the Pixel Helper icon, represented by the symbol </>, will appear on the upper-right corner of your browser. To download the Pixel Helper, follow these steps:

To test whether the pixels on your site are working, check if the Pixel Helper icon is green (firing correctly), yellow (error), gray (no pixel installed), or red (not firing).

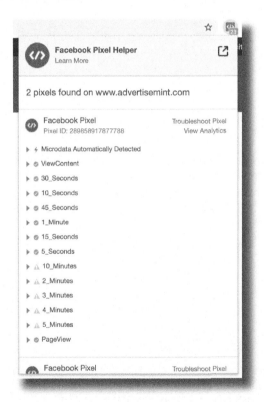

There are a few reasons your pixel is not working correctly. One, you installed the pixel for a purchase event, but you did not have a product catalog synced, causing your Pixel Helper to turn yellow. A yellow status means your pixel is still firing and collecting data, but there is an error with how a certain piece of information from your website is syncing with Facebook.

Two, your pixel was not installed correctly. If you do not immediately fix an incorrectly installed pixel, three scenarios can happen: one, no data transfers to Facebook; two, the pixel cannot track all users visiting your website; and three, tracking will be duplicated. If you click the pixel icon, you will see the information for debugging your pixel and the data your pixel has tracked.

People who have multiple pixels installed on their websites will often experience pixel problems. Although it is possible to have multiple fully functioning pixels on your site, problems may occur when all of your pixels do not load before your website fully loads.

ADS MANAGER MOBILE APP

The Ads Manager mobile app helps you manage and monitor your accounts while on the go. There are four features that make managing your accounts easier: the home page, the comparative view of your campaigns, a weekly summary, and recommended actions.

Home page: The home page contains quick-view summaries of your accounts, ads, and pages.

Campaigns: You can view several campaigns side by side to compare their metrics.

Weekly summary: The app also provides a weekly summary of your campaign performances, as well as other information about your ad account and creatives.

Recommended actions: The app will also recommend actions to help you improve your ad performance.

You can download the app from Google Play or the App Store.

FREQUENCY CAPPING WITH REACH

Frequency capping in reach campaigns is a strategy used by expert advertisers from big companies with big spends, like Coca-Cola, Capital One, or Geico, who want to consistently reach consumers. It is also a method advertisers from smaller companies use on their warmest audience.

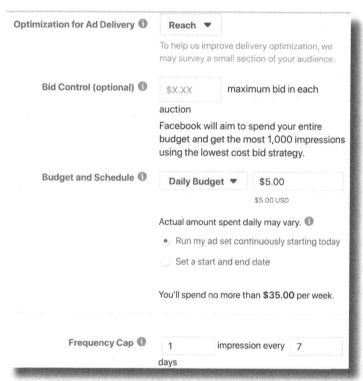

With frequency capping enabled in your reach campaigns, you can select a remarketing audience—for example, web visitors who accessed your website in the last 180 days or individuals who engaged with your business on Facebook or Instagram in the last 180 days—and set up specific campaigns to reach your core audience with one impression for every set number of days. With this method, you can ensure your brand stays top of mind for your customers while using a smaller ad budget. When you use frequency capping, remember to update your ads to prevent your audience from seeing your ads again and again.

THE SALES FUNNEL

There is one area that most Facebook advertisers struggle to understand or correctly implement: their sales funnel. Funnels can vary based on the specific nature of the business, but here is a general overview of the most common funnel structure for Facebook advertising.

Top of Funnel

This segment consists of individuals who know nothing about your company, product, or service. Your goal in this stage is to reach targeted new users at the lowest price possible and introduce your brand. One format you can use is a high-quality video, called an anchor video, that explains the benefits of your products or services to consumers in a fun, attention-grabbing way. You can also use contests, quizzes, or polls. These are great top-of-funnel content because they are not heavy on the sale and your audience does not perceive them as ads. Instead, top-of-funnel campaigns are designed to move a person further down the funnel at a low cost. Common ad objectives used for this stage are conversions (optimized for landing page views), video views, reach, and engagement.

When running a top-of-funnel campaign, you must exclude all website visitors, leads, email lists, people who engaged with your Facebook or Instagram ads, and customers. They are not the right type of audience for the introductory message you are sending. It is also important to know that top-of-funnel campaigns do not reap optimal ROAS. In fact, you should expect an estimated ROAS of 1%. Still, running this type of campaign is essential because it will help you push customers further down your funnel. Advertisers who skip this step often struggle with Facebook ads because the middle and bottom funnels should never be filled with new individuals. It should be filled with a warmer audience already familiar with the offers, products, and brand advertised.

Middle of Funnel

This segment consists of individuals who have shown interest in your product or service, whether by visiting your website or engaging with your ad. For this stage, your goal is to create desire for your product or service. This goal can rarely be achieved with a single ad. In fact, you must create ads that address the five reasons consumers will make a purchase: product, price, placement (where the ads appear), promotion (an enticing offer), and people (what people say about the product). For example, you can run an ad that features customer reviews for two weeks and run an ad promoting a sale in the next week. You can also use the common ad objectives for this stage, which are conversions (optimized for add to cart), lead generation, and branding. When running middle-of-funnel campaigns, you must exclude anyone in the bottom-of the-funnel segment, usually people who landed there in the past 7 to 15 days. You should also expect an estimated ROAS of 1 to 3%.

Bottom of Funnel

The bottom of the funnel is your smallest but best performing segment. These are composed of individuals who have recently visited your website or completed an action in the last 7 to 15 days—they are the users with the highest intent because they recently completed your targeted action. You need to move quickly to close the sale or complete the specific task the user left unfinished (for example, adding to cart but not checking out the items). Be prepared to bid very high to ensure your ads are shown first to these users. Your ads should be simple, providing clear offers, incentives, discounts, or promotions and creating a sense of urgency, a sense that the user should act immediately. You should expect an estimated ROAS of 3 to 10% from this segment and limited volume until you increase ad spend higher up on the funnel. This is also the first segment you should build when creating Facebook campaigns, as it will ensure you are capitalizing on the best-performing ads with the lowest costs from the beginning. When running bottom-of-funnel campaigns, use the objectives conversions (optimized for purchase), catalog sales, or lead generation.

Customers

This is the final segment and one that many advertisers forget, although it is a gold mine for several reasons. Because the individuals in the customers stage of your funnel have purchased or used your product or service, they are more likely to do so again in the future. They are also much more likely to leave comments on your ads, sharing stories about their experience, which are priceless forms of social proof. This audience segment is best to include in any holiday promotions, such as Black Friday, lead-generation campaigns, ads calling for product feedback, or any tests you run to see how certain ad creatives resonate with them. You should expect an estimated ROAS of 3 to 10% from this segment.

AD PLACEMENTS

Mobile News Feed

When you choose to place your ad on Facebook's mobile News Feed, your ad will appear on the app's News Feed. Much like desktop News Feed, your ad will appear among your friends and family's Facebook posts.

Some advertisers prefer placing their ads on mobile News Feed for two reasons. First, there is a higher likelihood that people will see the ad. Because mobile News Feed fills up an entire phone screen and posts appear on the screen one at a time, people have no choice but to look at your ad when it appears. Unlike the desktop News Feed, there is no left sidebar or right column to distract the eyes. Second, more people access Facebook through mobile.

This placement is eligible for the following objectives: brand awareness, reach, store traffic, engagement, app installs, video views, lead generation, conversions, messages, catalog sales, and store visits.

RIGHT COLUMN

The Facebook columns, also known as the right or left bars, appear on either side of your News Feed. The columns contain both important information and easily accessible actions. For example, the left column contains actions such as creating a Facebook event, an ad, or a fundraiser. The right column contains trending topics and Facebook ads. There are a few benefits to using the right column placement:

- Right Column Ads cannot be reported because the format does not support that feature.

- Right Column Ads usually work best with an older audience because that audience will often be more inclined to browse the entire page. A younger audience, in contrast, is extremely quick and impatient, often skimming through content at the speed of light. If your ad is not right in front of a young audience's eyes, it will most likely be missed.

- Right Column Ads are less intrusive than News Feed ads because they are separated from News Feed where people's posts appear.

When checking Facebook's News Feeds as your placement, the right column will automatically be included whether you want it or not. Facebook claims that it needs all placement options enabled to reach highly interested users at the lowest cost. Although this may be a reasonable explanation, remember that Facebook also profits from running ads in all of the placements regardless of whether that placement is the best for generating desired results. Test which placement works better for you.

AUDIENCE NETWORK

The Audience Network allows you to reach more people by placing ads on the apps and websites of Facebook's partners. The Audience Network offers three ad units: banner, interstitial, or native. You do not need to alter your ad creatives for these ad units because Facebook automatically renders your ad to fit the unit you choose.

Banner ads: Banner ads appear as banners on the lower part of the mobile screen.

Interstitial ads: These ads appear full-screen in users' mobile devices. They usually appear during pauses in games or during a natural break in an app's flow.

Native ads: Native ads seamlessly fit into any app that they appear in. They are customizable to the ad's appearance, size, and format.

If you are particular about brand safety, it is recommended that you exclude certain categories, or the type of content, you do not want your ads to appear in. The categories are dating, debatable social issues, gambling, mature, and tragedy and conflict. If there is a specific website or app you do not want your ad to be associated with, you can also create block lists.

TALK WITH AD EXPERT
This video explains the 3 biggest mistakes business owners make with their social ads.

LEARN MORE >

INSTAGRAM FEED

When you place your ad on Instagram's feed, your ad will appear among Instagram users' posts. You can place eligible Facebook ads on Instagram without reformatting your ads. Note that Instagram does not support all of Facebook's ad formats. Although Single Image, video, and Carousel Ads are eligible for placement on Instagram, Instant Experience Ads and Slideshow Ads are not.

If you want to tell your brand's story at the center of a visual representation, then consider placement on Instagram, a platform known for its visually focused content. To ensure that your ad successfully blends in with Instagram's environment, you must use professional, creative, high-quality, and visually appealing photos and videos for your ads. Take a few minutes to browse through brands' Instagram feeds to get acquainted with the type of content they usually post on Instagram.

INSTAGRAM STORIES

When you create ads, you can usually serve them to multiple placements. For example, you can place ads on Instagram's feed, Facebook's feed, and Audience Network simultaneously. That is not the case for placement on Stories. You cannot use other placements alongside Instagram Stories because those ads require specs that are incompatible with other ad formats and placements. For example, all Stories ads must be in a vertical video format. If you want to place ads on Instagram Stories, create separate creatives exclusively for that ad type.

MARKETPLACE

Marketplace is the buy-and-sell platform that Facebook launched in 2016. The platform was not open to advertising until 2018 when Facebook officially rolled out Marketplace as a placement.

Because Marketplace is a quasi e-commerce platform, it is recommended that you serve ads promoting products to this placement option. The categories in which your ads will appear include vehicles, clothing and accessories, entertainment, and electronics.

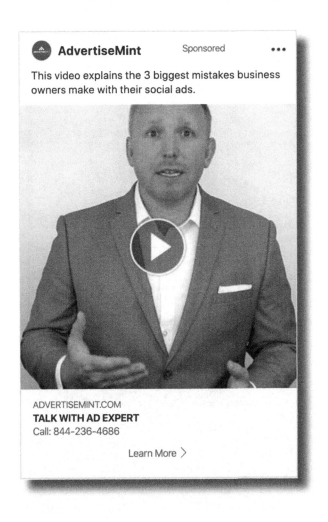

IN-STREAM VIDEO

You can place 5-to-15-second video ads within live and non-live videos on Facebook and Audience Network by choosing the in-stream video placement. Your in-stream video ad will display at the beginning, middle, or end of an online video.

When in-stream placement first launched, many advertisers felt apprehensive about using it because they were afraid their ads would appear within inappropriate content that they did not want associated with their brand. Content that was a cause for worry included adult, dating, and political content. If you do not want your ads to appear alongside certain types of content, you can include your block list in your ad or block certain categories as you would with placements on Audience Network.

Objectives eligible for this placement include brand awareness, engagement, video views, reach, app installs, lead generation, conversions, and catalog sales.

CREATING A BUYER PERSONA

It is not good practice to target an audience without identifying your ideal customers. Failing to understand the identity of your customers will result in targeting an audience too large, too expensive, and unlikely to convert. You must target the people who are most likely to be interested in your business. You can do this by creating a buyer persona that answers several questions about their identity, such as who they are, where they live, the languages they speak, their interests, and their purchasing habits.

Name	Janna Smith
Gender	Female
Age	30
Relationship Status	Never married
Location	Los Angeles
Income	$80K
Education	BA
Hobbies	Shopping, reading fashion magazines, going to the beach, hiking
Interests	Fashion, food, Malibu, nature, yoga
Story	Janna Smith is a single woman living in a one-bedroom apartment with her boyfriend in the greater Los Angeles area. She works as a marketing manager for a Facebook advertising agency. In her free time she works out, spends time with her boyfriend in the city, and goes shopping.

By answering questions about your customers' identity, you are creating a buyer persona, a fictional, generalized character that represents your ideal customers. This process helps you understand your buyers, create relevant ads, and better develop your ad targeting.

Advertisers usually conduct interviews to obtain the answers for their questions and create their buyer personas. However, those methods are time-consuming and costly. You would need to conduct interviews in a span of weeks, find and incentivize survey participants, and gather the data. The process could take up to a month. Fortunately, when you advertise on Facebook, you do not have to face those hurdles. You can, instead, create a buyer persona based on the information your Audience Insights provides. There you have all of the information you need: demographics, page likes, location, and activity.

LOCATION TARGETING

"Everyone in this location" is the default option. Choosing this broadens the scope of your targeting. Anyone at the location you choose will see your ad, whether those people are temporarily traveling to that area or living there permanently. Although a great option if you want to target a larger audience, it would not work as well if, for example, you want to drive foot traffic to your brick-and-mortar store. If you want to drive customers to your local business, "People who live in this location" is a better option for retaining long-term, local customers, "People recently in this location" for attracting customers who are nearby, and "People traveling in this location" for targeting tourists.

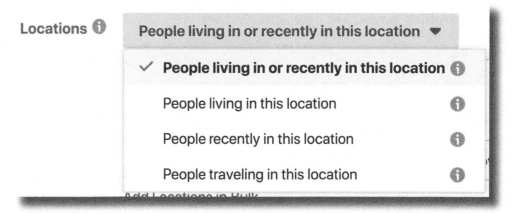

When setting the location for your ad, do not forget the available options that make your targeting more granular. You can choose the commonly used default option, or you can use the others if you have a specific audience that you want to target.

AGE TARGETING

There are certain rules to keep in mind when choosing the age of your target audience. First, you cannot target anyone under the age of 13 because that is the minimum age requirement to sign up for a Facebook account. This may be difficult for you if your business is suited for a younger audience. If you want to reach an audience younger than 13, you can target parents instead since they have the purchasing power.

Second, if you are selling alcohol globally, make sure to target the right drinking age for each respective country. You can do this by creating different ads. For example, create one ad targeting people aged 21 and over in the United States and one ad targeting people aged 18 and over in England. You can also create one ad for multiple countries, choosing the highest drinking age of them all. For example, if your ad targets the United States, where the legal drinking age is 21, and England, where the legal drinking age is 18, target users who are 21 and over because that is the highest drinking limit of the two. Of the two solutions, creating separate ads for each country is the best option because combining the counties in one ad will result in missing an age group. Using the England and U.S. example again, targeting only users who are aged 21 and over will cause you to miss the users who are aged 18 to 20.

DETAILED TARGETING

In certain cases, targeting demographics and behaviors may work better than targeting interests. If, for example, you want to target University of Colorado students, you can target by interests (users who liked University of Colorado's page) or by demographics (students who listed University of Colorado as their university in their profiles). However, if you target by interest, you may be targeting people who are not students of the University of Colorado. Although people liked the university's page, they are not necessarily students of that university. If you target by demographics, you are targeting people who are real students of the university.

If you want to get very detailed in your targeting and increase your chances of targeting an audience most likely to respond to your ads, use the Connections option, which allows you to target only the people who have a specific connection to your business. You can target people who liked your page, who used your app, or who attended your event. You can even exclude connections if you want to reach new customers.

Although Facebook gives you numerous options to make your targeting as detailed as possible, do not make your targeting too detailed. An ad with targeting that is too detailed will result in an audience that is too narrow to be effective. Instead, try to achieve a happy medium and refer to your audience meter. The happy medium is in the middle of the green arch.

CUSTOM AUDIENCES

Custom Audiences is particularly helpful in achieving three goals:

1. It can garner more conversions by targeting users who are already in your customer list, who have proven to be loyal customers, and who are already interested in your business. In contrast, if you no longer want to advertise to the people in your list (such a situation would occur if you were to create a brand awareness campaign targeting only those who have never interacted with your business), you can exclude your Custom Audience from your target audience.

2. You can use Custom Audiences to build a Lookalike Audience, which would allow you to target new users who are similar to your current customers.

3. You can use Custom Audiences for remarketing, serving ads to users who committed specific actions on your website or Facebook page and posts.

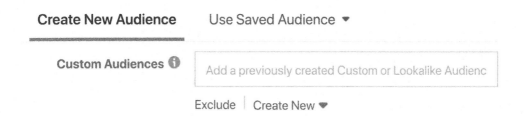

A Custom Audience is important to have. As you create one Custom Audience after another, keep those three use cases in mind.

MULTI-COUNTRY LOOKALIKE AUDIENCE

If you want to target users from a different country, it is recommended that you run a Worldwide Lookalike Audience. To do so, you must upload a Lookalike Audience and choose the countries where you want Facebook to find similar users. Facebook will take the audience you provide and search for similar audiences within the country that you choose, based on qualities such as interests and demographics.

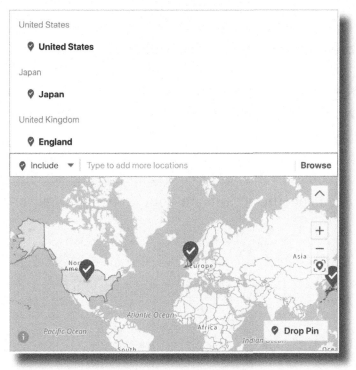

For best results, upload an audience containing 1,000 to 50,000 individuals with the highest lifetime value, order size, or engagement. An audience containing individuals from the country where you want to expand your reach also helps the performance of your ad. For example, an audience with users from Germany will help your ad perform better if you set the ad to appear in that country. If you do not know the country where you audience resides, you can improve your ad's performance by enlarging your audience. A larger audience gives Facebook enough diversity to find a match with the best similarities.

INTERESTS VS BEHAVIORS

There are hundreds of options for detailed targeting, which includes hobbies and activities, entertainment, business and industry, sports, shopping, fashion, food and drink, fitness, and wellness. You can target certain interests and behaviors by typing the keyword in the detailed targeting search box.

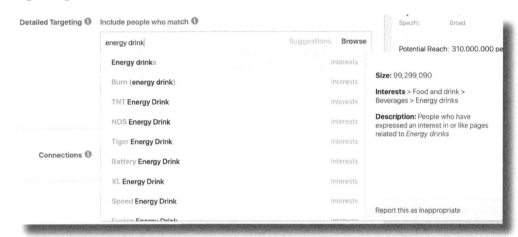

You can differentiate between a suggestion that is under the interests category and a suggestion that is under the demographics category by looking at the category label next to the suggestions. If an interest-targeting option, the suggestion should be labeled "interests." Target audiences differ according to different targeting categories. For example, if you typed "energy drinks" and clicked an interest-targeting option, Facebook will send the ad to people who expressed interest in energy drinks on Facebook (e.g., following or liking an energy drink page). If, instead, you clicked a behavior-targeting option, Facebook will send the ad to people who are known to be or likely to be buyers of energy drinks based on their purchase behavior. To ensure you are targeting the people you want, check that the option you are choosing is from the correct category.

AUDIENCE SIZE

You can target people of any purchase behavior, any interest, and in any location, whether that is in the United States, Canada, or the Philippines. Facebook's targeting almost has no limits.

Facebook created targeting options from self-reported data, which comes from the information users provide on their profiles, such as occupation, education, relationship status, and interests. Facebook used to provide third-party data for ad targeting, but after the Cambridge Analytica scandal, in which an app misused millions of users' personal information for political ad targeting, the company decided to remove data from third parties. Despite this change, Facebook's targeting is still effective in targeting an audience most likely to respond to ads.

With Facebook's vast targeting options, you will likely try to target as many users as you can. Do not do that. Bigger is not always better, and that adage rings true for ad targeting. When you target an audience, the median is key. Make sure your audience is neither too broad nor too narrow. The former can result in targeting people who are not interested in your business, while the latter can result in excluding high-interest, potential customers. To check whether your audience is too big or too small, refer to the audience-size meter that appears on the right side of your screen.

Audience Size

Your audience selection is fairly broad.

Specific   Broad

Potential Reach: 310,000,000 people ⓘ

Your criteria is currently set to allow detailed targeting expansion. ⓘ

CONNECTIONS

You can also target users according to their connection with your business. You can target users or friends of those users who liked your Facebook pages, used your apps, or responded to your events. Conversely, you can exclude anyone who has any connections with your business.

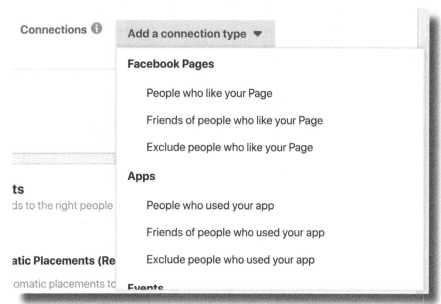

Connections is best used to reach new customers who are likely to be interested in your business. A user who responded to one of your events, for example, has shown an interest. Because of this interest, that user is most likely to be receptive to the ads you run.

Connections is also best used to exclude an audience on the brink of experiencing ad fatigue or users who already responded to your offer. For example, if you are running an ad to promote your event, you can exclude users who already RVSPed. This not only prevents wasting money on users who already converted, but it also prevents users from growing tired of your ads.

ACQUIRING NEW CUSTOMERS

If you want to acquire new customers who are most likely to be interested in your business, target a Lookalike Audience. One issue you may encounter when targeting a Lookalike Audience is this: It is very broad. For that reason you may need to narrow your audience by pairing your Lookalike Audience with detailed targeting. You can, for example, include targeting details related to interests. Refer to the audience-size meter to see whether your audience is too narrow or too broad.

You can also acquire new customers by using Broad Audience Targeting with exclusions. You exclude people who interacted with your business, liked your page, interacted with your app, or responded to your event.

SETTING UP REMARKETING

Because customers normally deliberate for a few days before buying, it is often beneficial to set up remarketing to push customers to purchase, to encourage them to revisit the product that captured their attention. Remarketing is also effective and cost-efficient because it reaches customers who are already in the bottom of the sales funnel.

Remarketing ads usually appear to users for 30 days. After 30 days, the ads automatically stop displaying. To create a remarketing ad, choose any objective with any ad format and go to the ad set level. From there you must select the Custom Audience option for your targeting.

After you choose your retargeting option, pick your schedule. Although you can retarget for 30 days, retarget with different ads to avoid ad fatigue. For example, create an ad for customers who visited your website in the last one to three days, then another for four to seven days. When you do this, customers will see the first ad for three days, then the second ad for four to seven days. Make sure to tweak your ads slightly so your customers are not repeatedly seeing the same one.

Once your customers convert, it is good practice to exclude them from your remarketing ads. If your customers bought the product you have been advertising for the past month, it is highly unlikely that they will purchase the same product again. As a result, you will waste money serving ads to people who are not going to convert.

To exclude an audience, follow these steps:

Step 1: In Business Manager, go to **Audience > Create a Custom Audience > Website Traffic > Purchase**.

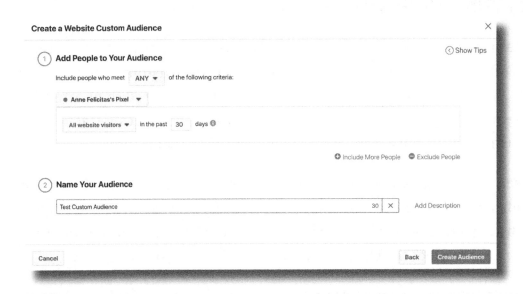

Step 2: Go to the ad set level. Click Exclude and select your purchase Custom Audience.

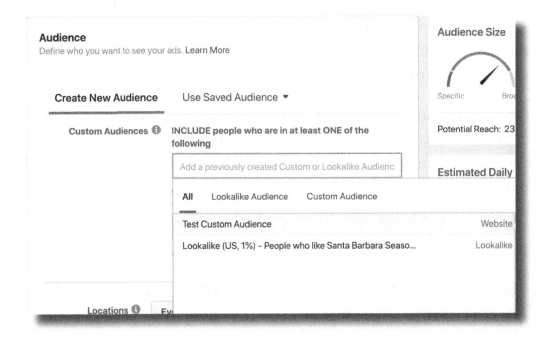

LEAD ADS

Lead Ads collect valuable information from potential customers without directing them outside of Facebook's platform. From phone numbers to email addresses to job titles, Lead Ads collect any information you want from your potential leads.

Lead Ads are superior to website forms for two reasons. First, Lead Ads were built with the mobile user in mind. Because the forms open directly in Facebook's app, users will never leave the app. Instead, they can quickly complete your mobile-friendly form from their devices rather than from a web page that may load too slowly on a mobile phone. Second, Lead Ads automatically prefill the forms with users' profile information. This pre-filled form enables a user to accurately complete and submit a response within seconds.

There are several best practices to keep in mind when creating your Lead Ad. When you set your budget, optimize for leads rather than link clicks. Choosing the latter may result in a higher click-through rate. Although your Lead Ad is eligible for the carousel, single-image, single-video, and slideshow formats, use the single-image format to avoid losing a lead. Because you want the process to finish as quickly as possible, keep your form simple and easy.

Budget & Schedule
Define how much you'd like to spend, and when you'd like your ads to appear.

Optimization for Ad Delivery ❶   **Leads** - We'll show your ads to the right people to help you get the most leads.

Write copy that gives your audience a clear understanding of your business and your offer. Disclose what your customers will get in return (if anything) for their contact information. When you create your form, keep your questions to a minimum. Lengthy forms may dissuade your customers from completing the form. Only ask for what you need. If you must ask questions on your form, ask multiple-choice questions rather than open-ended questions. A convenient process leads to more conversions.

After running your Lead Ads for a few days, you can then compile the information you obtained into a spreadsheet that you later upload to your Custom Audience. Afterward, use your Custom Audience to remarket to the customers who responded to your Lead Ad.

Full name	Enter your answer.
Email	Enter your answer.
Phone number	US +1 ▼ Enter your answer.
Street address	Enter your answer.
City	Enter your answer.
Zip code	US ▼ Enter your answer.

Cancel   Next

CREATING CONDITIONAL ANSWERS

Conditional answers in Lead Ad forms automatically change according to users' previous responses. For example, if your form asked users for their country, and users answered "United States," the answers in the next question will change based on the response "United States." If the next question asked users for the state where they reside, the form will then give states within the United States as the options because of the answer to the previous question.

To create a Lead Ad form with conditional answers, follow these steps:

Step 1: Choose the Lead Generation objective, go to the ad level, click **New Form**.

Step 2: Click **Questions > Custom Questions > Add Custom Question > Conditional**.

Step 3: Upload spreadsheet.

Step 4: Write the questions. Word them in a way that is applicable to all of the possible answers.

USING THE AD LIBRARY

Facebook created the Ad Library to provide transparency behind its advertising. Facebook is the first and only social media ad platform that helps users find and view all running and paused ads in one location. In the past, this type of information would cost thousands of dollars per business to access, but with Facebook, it is available at no charge.

You can view the ads library online:

facebook.com/ads/library

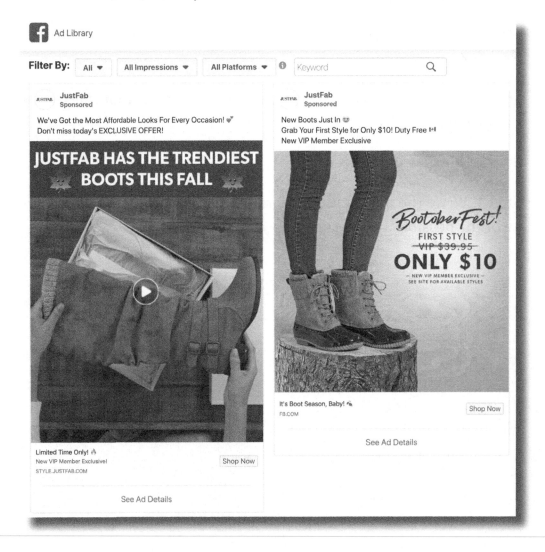

You can use the Ad Library for two purposes:

1. To quickly find and share a link of all the ads you are currently running for review by a boss, co-worker, or agency.

2. To view any ads that competitors are running. You can use the Ad Library to gain ideas for your next ads or to find ways to improve them. When analyzing your competitors' ads, make sure to look closely at the ad copy, headline, ad format (image, video, Carousel, Instant Experience), and layout (horizontal, square, or vertical). Taking inspiration from other high-quality ads is one of the best ways to improve your campaign results.

SHARING YOUR FACEBOOK ADS

You may need to share your ads with others. For example, you way want to show your ad to a colleague for feedback or to your boss or client for approval. To share your Facebook ads, follow the steps below:

Step 1: Go to Ads Manager, select an ad, click Preview (located on the top menu bar), then click the box and arrow icon next to "Ad Preview." Click Share Link.

Step 2: Copy the URL provided and share it with anyone who needs access. This ad will now be viewable to anyone with the link. The individual can then click the Show Ad button, which will show the ad in users' Instagram or Facebook feeds.

USING UTM PARAMETERS

UTM parameters attach to the end of a URL and pass critical information to your analytics. They allow you to determine the source of an action, for example, a visit to your website. The most commonly used tool to access data from your UTM parameters is Google Analytics. Go to Google Analytics > Acquisition > All Traffic > Source/Medium.

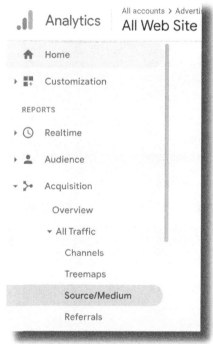

You can track five types of URL parameters:

  » **Campaign source:** Where the traffic came from
  » **Campaign medium:** The type of traffic the action came from (e.g., email, referral, social)
  » **Campaign name:** The type of campaign the traffic came from (e.g., Facebook ad, email campaign)
  » **Campaign content:** Used to differentiate which ad was clicked

There are two ways you can attach UTM parameters to your links within Facebook.

FACEBOOK UTM BUILDER

In the ad level of Ads Manager, under the section **Text and Links**, there is an option to Build a **URL Parameter**. Click this, and you will be prompted to enter the landing page URL and the details for source, medium, name, and content.

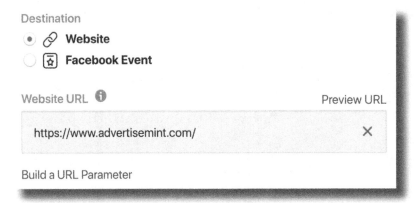

If you use Google Analytics for reporting, it is recommended that you keep everything lowercase. Facebook also gives you the option to select the ID or name of any campaign, ad set, or ad. This is a quick way to add the information dynamically so you can track the results later on.

GOOGLE UTM BUILDER

Google also has an option to quickly create UTM variables on its Campaign URL Builder online tool.

URL Builder:

https://ga-dev-tools.appspot.com/campaign-url-builder/

* Website URL	
	The full website URL (e.g. `https://www.example.com`)
* Campaign Source	
	The referrer: (e.g. `google` , `newsletter`)
* Campaign Medium	
	Marketing medium: (e.g. `cpc` , `banner` , `email`)
* Campaign Name	
	Product, promo code, or slogan (e.g. `spring_sale`)
Campaign Term	
	Identify the paid keywords
Campaign Content	
	Use to differentiate ads

Simply enter all of your data, then copy the link and paste it into the URL field of your Facebook ad. You can use the UTM variables to create Custom Audiences. This means if you are paying a high price for targeted users through Google CPC campaigns, you can create a Custom Audience of any user who visited a URL with "utm_source=google" at the end of the link and ensure those users go into a higher-priority ad campaign.

FINDING DELETED ADS

When campaigns have run their course, many advertisers delete them so they no longer appear. However, this causes issues when the advertiser is looking through past data and trying to get an accurate measure of past performance. To find deleted ads, go to Ads Manager and click Filters on the upper-left corner. Then click **Campaign Delivery > Deleted**. You will be able to view any campaigns, ad sets, and ads that have been deleted. Because you cannot turn on deleted campaigns, you must first duplicate them, then run the duplicates as new ads.

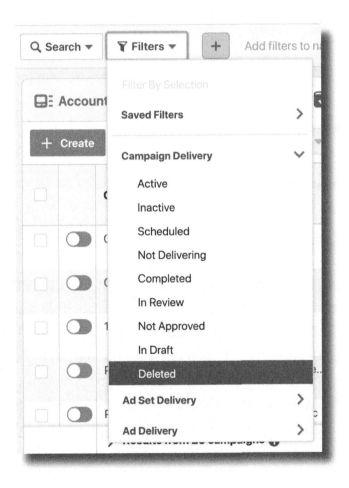

FIXING UNDERPERFORMING ADS

A time may come when your ads underperform. Here are a few ways you can improve them.

Low Click-Through Rates

If you notice that your CTR is low, refresh your creatives by changing the ad's media, copy, or format. If your creatives are not resonating with your audience, then it is time to create a new ad that will resonate. If that solution does not work, change your audience. If your ad is not resonating with your target audience, it is likely because you are targeting the wrong one. In this case, target people who are most likely to respond to your message, such as current customers and Lookalikes.

High Cost per Click

Pause or change your ad if your CPC is too high. Of course, a CPC that is "too high" varies from industry to industry and client to client. For example, a client who spends $50 per link click likely will not be too bothered if the returns are in the thousands. To determine whether your CPC is too high, look at your ROAS and ask yourself this: "Am I paying too much for the return that I'm getting?" If the answer is yes, change your ad.

Low Impressions

Low impressions is a sign that your bid is too low. If your bid is low, your competitors can outbid you for a spot on News Feed. Consequently, your ad will appear to a fewer number of users, resulting in fewer impressions. When this happens, increase your bid.

High Cost per Impressions

Use CPM to determine whether your ad is relevant to your audience. A high CPM can be a sign that Facebook deems your ad irrelevant to your audience. If that is the case, Facebook would display your ad to fewer users, resulting in fewer impressions. If your CPM is high, change your audience. Ideally, target an audience most likely to be interested in your business, such as Lookalikes or people in your Custom Audience.

Low Relevance Score

If you notice that your results and relevance score are declining while your frequency is increasing, it is a sign that your audience is experiencing ad fatigue. When this happens, you must change your ad creatives or targeting.

Low Reach

If your reach is low, fewer users are seeing your ads. Your bid, budget, and audience targeting can affect your reach. If you have a large audience with a low reach, increase your bids because competitors are outbidding you for a spot in your chosen placement.

ADDRESSING TECHNICAL AD ISSUES

Ads Stuck in Review

Before they can be published for your audience to see, Facebook ads must first pass the review phase. Although the review process finishes within a few minutes, it can take up to 48 hours for an ad to be approved. Your ads may take longer to be approved if the account is new and does not have a history of consistent ad spend or if the ad account has a history of disapproved ads or policy violations. Ads are often screened by the algorithm for violations. If the ad is flagged by the system, it will either be rejected or sent to a human for further review. If you feel like your ad is stuck in the review process and seems never to be approved, you can take three courses of action:

Action 1: Go to Ads Manager and find the ad. Click the **Request Manual Review** link. This will re-submit the ad for human review.

Action 2: Duplicate the ad and then publish. Often, the second ad (if it does not violate ad policies) will be approved without any issues.

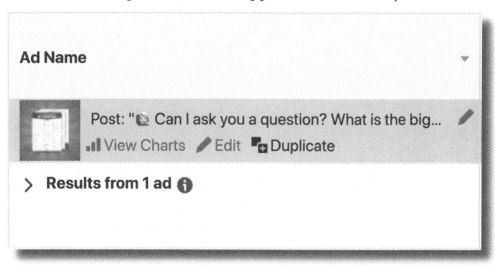

Action 3: Contact Facebook's support team at **facebook.com/business/resources**.

AD DISAPPROVALS

An ad is disapproved when it violates Facebook's ad policy or when users reported your ad to Facebook. When this happens, Facebook will let you know which part of the ad policy your ad violated. You will need to update the ad to remove any violations and then resubmit. This can often be a frustrating process because some ads fall into a gray area. If you believe your ad is within the ad policy guidelines, you can request a manual review or contact the Facebook support team.

Facebook support team:

https://www.facebook.com/help/contact/1582364792025146

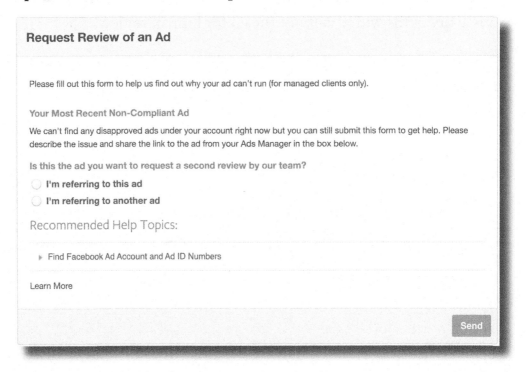

AD ACCOUNT BLOCKED OR DISABLED

Your ad account may be blocked or disabled if it has historically violated Facebook's ad policy or if it appears as a malicious account to Facebook's system. Even the slightest mistake or a non-compliant experiment can lead to a blocked or disabled ad account. Facebook wants to prevent advertisers from causing harm to or negative experiences for its users. If suspicious activity is detected, Facebook would rather block an account first, and then fix an incorrect or unfair decision later. It is important to understand why and how Facebook blocks accounts and what you can do to get your campaigns running again.

Because all account activities are linked, the new accounts you create after your first account has been blocked or disabled will appear as suspicious accounts to Facebook's system. Those accounts will be flagged, and Facebook's team will monitor them closely for any violation. Your payment method—whether a debit or credit card—is also linked between accounts. Although you may have one violating ad account and one compliant ad account, both could still be blocked because they come from the same billing source. If your business violates one of Facebook's ad policies, you will most likely be unable to advertise on Facebook. Although Facebook will sometimes make exceptions, the process of coming to a final decision is a slow one. If your ad account has been blocked or disabled, you can request an appeal.

FACEBOOK CONTACT FOR APPEALS

https://www.facebook.com/help/contact/391647094929792

Disabled Payments & Ads Manager

If you believe your ad account was disabled by mistake, you can request a review. Please provide more information to help us understand what's going on.

Who is the owner of the Ad Account?

Select Disabled Ad Account

No Advertising Account ▼

Please let us know if any of these conditions apply

○ **Country of your credit and/or debit cards doesn't match your current location**

○ **You've recently been traveling**

○ **You've recently relocated**

You can add more info to help us understand why you believe your account should be restored.

If you are unable to submit this form please click here.

Send

ADVERTISING BEST PRACTICES

Keeping Audiences Fresh

To avoid wearing out your audience, target a different group by creating a Lookalike Audience and building remarketing campaigns that target only people who clicked your ad without performing your desired action.

If your ad is not performing well, it may be because your audience is worn out. If you keep sending ads to the same audience over and over again, that audience may grow tired of your offer. In a different case, the offer is no longer relevant to them because they already converted. To know whether or not your audience is worn out, look at the first-time impressions-ratio metric from the delivery tab under the ad set level. That metric will give you the percentage of users who are seeing your ad for the first time. If that metric is below 50%, most of the individuals in your audience have already seen your ad.

You can also keep current audiences interested by refreshing your ads. If you do not refresh your ads by changing your media and copy at least every two weeks, your audience will suffer from ad fatigue and your relevance score will plummet.

Diversifying Your Placements

Placing your ads on more placement options will help you optimize your results. For this reason, automatic placements is a better option than manual placements. With the former option, Facebook will serve your ads to the placements where it determines they will fulfill your objective for the lowest cost. Do not be afraid to experiment with ad placements and to find the one that works best.

Choosing the Right Conversion Window

When creating an ad with the conversion objective, instead of choosing the one-day click conversion window, try the seven-day window. By choosing the seven-day window, you are telling Facebook to send your ad to people who are likely to purchase within seven days, which is enough time for people to see your ad, contemplate, and purchase. Often, customers do not buy the first time they see your ad. Rather, they may take some time to deliberate.

LANDING PAGE BEST PRACTICES

You may not realize that Facebook scans the landing page of your ads. Although your ads may not violate the social media company's ad policies, those ads may still be disapproved if their landing pages are non-compliant. Here are a few tips to ensure your landing pages do not violate Facebook's ad policies:

1. Do not make claims you cannot prove with research.

2. Do not create a landing page that redirects to other pages.

3. The products and services promoted in the ad must match those in your landing page.

4. The landing page must not contain too many ads.

5. Do not include excessive before-and-after images.

6. The landing page must be fully functional.

7. The landing page must comply with Facebook's ad policies.

8. The landing page must not stop or prevent users from leaving the website.

9. Make sure your landing page does not contain spammy or low-quality content.

10. All financial and insurance ads must have disclosures in the landing page.

11. Landing pages must not contain Facebook's copyrights and trademarks.

CUSTOMER FEEDBACK SCORE

Few advertisers are aware of The Customer Feedback Score. It is important to understand this tool because failure to monitor can lead to an increase in ad costs.

Within 30 to 60 days after purchase, a randomly selected group of customers will receive a survey in their News Feeds, inviting them to rate their recent purchase experience. The survey will ask customers about the product quality, shipping speed, and customer service. Facebook will determine your Customer Feedback Score based on customers' ratings. A number from one to five (one being the lowest score and five being the highest), your Customer Feedback Score can be accessed online.

View Your Customer Feedback Score
https://business.facebook.com/ads/customer_feedback

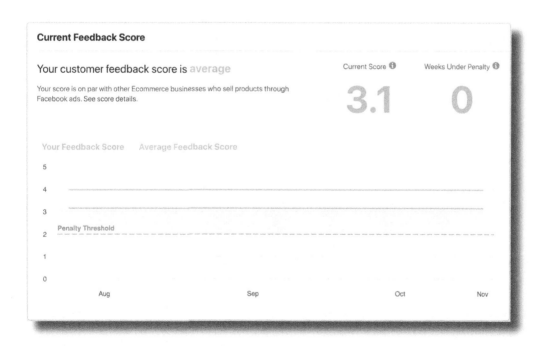

If your score falls below two, you will receive an email warning you of your account's penalty status. Once your account is under penalty, your ad's reach may be restricted and the amount you pay for ads may increase. Keep in mind that your Customer Feedback Score has nothing to do with the quality of your ads. It is based on the feedback Facebook receives from customers. If your business has slow shipping times, poor customer service, or low-quality products, you will receive a low feedback score and have a difficult time advertising on Facebook.

Fortunately, you can improve your feedback score with a few changes:

1. Make sure your products or services are accurately advertised.

2. Make sure your products are shipped on time.

3. Make sure your products do not take too long to arrive.

4. Make it easy for customers to return or exchange their purchases.

5. Do not advertise products that are low in inventory.

AD CREATIVES

Adding a Poll to Your Videos

Facebook has a feature that allows you to create polls within videos. This feature can help you increase the engagement on your published videos and improve the performance of your video marketing campaigns.

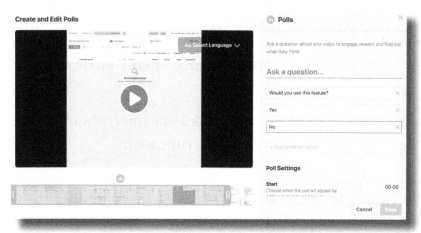

To add a poll to your videos, follow the steps below:

Step 1: Go to your Facebook page. Click **Create Post** then **Photo/Video**. Upload a video.

Step 2: Fill in the required fields in the upload screen, then click **Polls** in the menu on the right.

Step 3: Create your poll question and answers.

Step 4: Set the time when your poll will appear and disappear from your video.

Step 5: Choose whether or not viewers can see poll results.

Step 6: Click **Save Poll**.

The poll will appear for however long you choose. A question will appear over your video, which users can click to answer the options provided.

OPTIMIZING CREATIVE FOR MOBILE

Images

1. **Use vibrant, eye-catching images**. Your ad competes against content posted in News Feeds. Make sure your image stands out.

2. **Turn images into slideshows**. To capture attention, turn a series of images into slideshows using Facebook's Slideshow ad format.

3. **Keep it simple**. A busy image will not display well on a smaller screen.

Copy

Make sure your ad copy is short. Because smartphones have smaller screens, most of your ad copy will be truncated.

Video

1. **Make sure it is short**, with a length of three minutes at the most. Users will not likely watch the entirety of your video if it is too long.

2. **Place the story's important message within the first few seconds of the ad**. Because viewers scroll out of a video if it has not captured their attention within the first 15 seconds, it is crucial that you hook your viewers and communicate your message immediately. Treat your videos like a news article, following the pyramid format: Use the most important points first, followed by the least important points. While doing so, make sure that your video still makes logical sense according to your story. It should still be cohesive despite the inversion.

3. **Create your videos for sound off** because most users watch without sound. You can cater to those users by adding subtitles or including captions that encourage your viewers to watch with sound on.

4. **Make sure that your video's story is easily comprehensible** even without captions or sound.

5. **Use the vertical or square format**. These formats fill in the screen.

INSTAGRAM STORIES ADS

Instagram Stories ads are 10-to 15-second, full-screen vertical video ads that appear between Instagram users' Stories, videos, or photos and disappear from the Stories bar after 24 hours. Although this ad is exclusive to Instagram, you can create it only in Facebook's Ads Manager.

To succeed on the platform, follow these tips:

1. **Make It Relevant.** Ads that are relevant to your audience perform well on average. When creating your Instagram Stories ads, make sure that the content is relatable to the audience you are targeting.

2. **Keep It Short.** Keep your video length at 15 seconds. Exceed that length, and you will lose your audience's interest. Because your video has to be short, make sure your main point appears at the beginning of the ad.

3. **Design for Sound Off but Delight with Sound.** People usually view Stories with sound on. Thus, use delightful music that people will enjoy hearing, but also design videos for sound off in case users decide to turn off their volumes.

4. **Use Fast-Paced Videos.** If your Stories ad contains more than one scene or clip, edit the clips together to make a fast-paced video. Top-performing ads, on average, include brief clips with quick scenes.

5. **Experiment with Instagram's Creative Tools**

Create eye-catching and engaging Stories by using Instagram's tools, such as Poll, Quizzes, Pens, and Stickers.

COMMON HEADLINE TEMPLATES

If certain headline formats have historically worked for you, do not hesitate to reuse them. Here are a few common headline templates you can use for your ads:

How to: *How to remove carpet stains in 3 seconds.*

Listicle: *Five ways to quickly remove carpet stains.*

Who wants [this benefit]?: *Who else wants an easy way to get rid of carpet stains?*

Unlock the secret of: Unlock the secret of removing carpet stains in 3 seconds.

Here is a method that is helping [your target audience] to [a helpful benefit]: *Here is a method that is helping moms quickly and easily remove carpet stains.*

Unknown ways to [solve a problem]: *Here are little known ways to remove carpet stains in 3 seconds.*

Get rid of [a problem]: *Get rid of those pesky carpet stains once and for all.*

Here's a quick way to [solve a problem]: *Here's a quick way to remove carpet stains.*

Now you can [have something desirable]: Now you can quit your job and make even more money.

[Do something] like [an expert]: Remove carpet stains like Mr. Clean.

Have a [blank] you can be proud of: *Have a clean carpet you can be proud of.*

Build a [blank] you can be proud of: *Build a career you can be proud of.*

What everybody needs to know about [blank]: *What everybody needs to know about removing carpet stains.*

AD COPY SPECIFICATIONS

Your ad copy will appear in three areas of your ad: as the text above the image, as the headline under the image, and as the description under the headline. The text appears above the image, usually containing details about your product or service, a value proposition, and a CTA. The text should convey everything your audience needs to know about the ad. What does it offer? What should your audience expect upon clicking the ad?

It is important to know the text specification for those three areas. If your copy is too long, your text will be truncated. Here are Facebook's ad copy requirements:

Format: Videos, Single Images, Slideshows
Text: 125 characters

Headline: 25 characters

Link description: 30 characters

Format: Collection
Text: 90 characters

Headline: 25 characters

Format: Carousel
Text: 125 characters

Headline: 40 characters

Format: Dynamic Product Ads
Text: 255 characters

Although fewer characters are often recommended by advertisers and copywriters alike, you are more than welcome to write longer text. As always, split test to find the text length that garners the best results.

IMAGES

The image is the most important, most dominant part of your ad because, due to its large size, it is the first element users see. When choosing the image of your ad, keep these tips in mind:

1. **Avoid stock images.** Stock images have often been used by other advertisers. Create your own images to make your ads unique to your brand.

2. **Add text on the image.** The image receives the most attention. You can add your marketing message or call to action to your image by including text overlays. Make sure the text does not dominate the image; otherwise, Facebook will not approve your ad.

3. **Feature recognizable people in your images.** Ads that feature people your target audience recognizes, such as a celebrity, perform better than ads that feature unrecognizable people. If possible, work with an influencer, public figure, or celebrity to add more credibility to your ads.

4. **Feature the logo of partners** if possible. For example, if the software you advertise integrates with Gmail, ManyChat, and Microsoft, include those companies' logos to add credibility to your services.

5. **Feature product shots** if you are creating ads for e-commerce. This will help set expectations as to what customers can expect when they receive your product.

6. **Feature models using your product.** This shows customers the functionality of the items you are advertising. It also allows them to visualize how they may be able to use the product. The Carousel Ad is the best format for this purpose.

EDUCATE, ENTERTAIN, ENGAGE

When building your creatives, remember to entertain, educate, and engage. This strategy may help your ads attract the attention of your target audience, increase brand lift, and encourage engagement.

Entertain

Social media users do not go to Facebook to shop. Rather, they go to Facebook to be entertained. To catch your audience's attention, make sure your ads make people smile, laugh, or cry. Make them experience love, wonder, mystery, or fear.

Educate

Teaching people something they did not know, such as a new skill or a little-known fact, is the second tactic to improving your results. Educating your audience works well because you give users something in return for their time and attention: knowledge and a solution. Create content that educates your customers about your products and shows them how your offerings are the best solutions to their problems.

Engage

Make sure your ad engages your audience. For example, in an Instagram Stories ad, include a poll or a quiz to encourage interaction. On Facebook, you can run Instant Experience Ads or Carousel Ads, which users can click and scroll through. Engagement matters to Facebook's algorithm, as it signals that your ad is relevant to your users.

THE 5 P'S OF MARKETING

There are several reasons people purchase, reasons that are often referred to in marketing books as the five P's. The five P's are product, price, placement, promotion, and people. If used correctly, the five P's can push your customers to convert.

Product

Customers will most likely purchase from you when you offer a superior product or service that meets their needs. Let us say a customer is considering buying two cars that are identical in size, color, and speed. However, one car gets 25 miles to the gallon and the other gets 50 miles to the gallon. If that customer has long commutes, she will most likely purchase the car with the better gas mileage. When it comes to Facebook ads, you need to show customers that your product or service is better than that of your competitors'.

Price

Customers will also most likely purchase from you if your product is fairly priced, especially in comparison to your competitors. If your and your competitors' products are similar in appearance, type, and functionality, customers will most likely purchase the product with the lowest price. It is important that you sell a product with a competitive price, especially when customers can easily compare online.

Placement

Another element that compels customers to buy is placement, or the location of your product. The strategic placement of your Facebook ad is key. For example, if you own multiple brick-and-mortar stores, you can create Store Traffic Ads to target people within your store location, or you can place ads in areas that your audience frequently visits, whether that is on mobile News Feed, desktop News Feed, or right column.

Promotion

Promotions create a sense of urgency and exclusivity, causing customers to hastily purchase. Imagine you are shopping for a new credit card. You find two cards with the same APR, same spending limit, and same travel points. However, one card charges you 0% interest on purchases for the first 18 months. You would choose the 0% APR credit card, of course, because it is a better deal. Offering a promotion can often be a strong tactic to drive customers to purchase your product rather than your competitors' products.

People

"People" pertains to friends' and public figures' influence on someone's purchasing decision. Customers are more likely to purchase a product when it has been recommended or praised by friends, family, a public figure, or a celebrity. Recommendations and praise from these people are called social proof, and you can incorporate it into your ads by featuring customer reviews or acquiring more ad engagement.

THE BEFORE-AND-AFTER EFFECT

For your ads to be effective, make sure they are relevant, providing solutions to customers' problems. See the before-and-after chart:

	Before Your Product (Dish Soap)	After Your Product (Dish Soap)
Your Customers Have	Dirty Dishes	Clean Dishes
Your Customers Feel	Frustrated	Accomplished
Your Customers' Average Day	Tiring	Productive
Your Customers' Status	Failure	Winner

Your ad should illustrate the state of your audience before your product or service and after your product or service. Examine the example copy below.

Your Customers Have
Tired of dirty dishes? Get **squeaky clean** *dishes with Miracle soap.*

Your Customers Feel
Hard-to-wash dirty dishes can <u>frustrate you</u>. *With Miracle soap,* **you'll feel accomplished** *after every washing session.*

Your Customers' Average Day
Every day is exhausting when you spend too much time scrubbing hard-to-clean dishes. Miracle soap will leave you **feeling productive** *at the end of the day.*

Your Customers' Status
Not getting the grease off of your dishes may leave you <u>feeling like a failure</u>. *Easily scrub that grease away with Miracle soap.* **Feel like a winner.**

EVOKING EMOTIONS

On average, a user will view your ad on a mobile News Feed for 1.7 seconds and for 2.5 seconds on a desktop News Feed. If you want to compel your audience, instill a sense of urgency, kinship, or difficulty.

Urgency

Creating a sense of urgency is one of the best ways to compel a user to complete a desired action. There is one emotion that makes the urgency tactic effective: fear. People fear a lost opportunity and regret. When creating your ad, play into customers' fear of missing out by instilling a sense of urgency.

Scarcity

When people think a product is in low supply, they feel compelled to take action, fearing the loss of the item. Scarcity tactics often work well alongside sales or discounts that provide the benefit of buying your product. Although scarcity tactics can increase sales, it is wise not to overuse them because customers will become skeptical and, consequently, doubtful of your business.

Difficulty

Free giveaways may ring false to your customers because they may think it is too good to be true. To alleviate customers' skepticism, offer free items as an incentive to take a certain action, for example, following your page or taking your short survey. Doing so gives skeptics a realistic offer that will allay their doubts.

Kinship

To be more relatable to your customers, show that you understand their needs. For example, if promoting security equipment, express the importance of protecting one's property and family. Then, present your product as the solution.

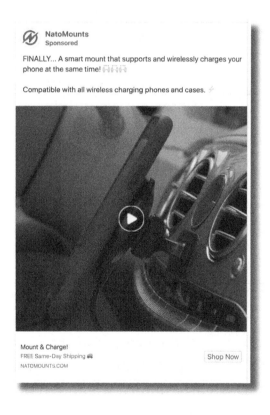

THE PSYCHOLOGICAL IMPACT OF COLORS

Color evokes feelings and emotions that can influence your audience's state of mind. You can use certain colors to better deliver your marketing message to your target audience. For example, if you are promoting your spa, you can use creatives that predominantly use the color blue. The chart below contains the emotions and symbolism certain colors evoke.

Yellow	optimism, clarity, youthfulness, warmth, cheerfulness
Orange	friendship, cheerfulness, confidence, warmth, intuition, optimism, spontaneity, cordiality, freedom, impulsiveness, motivation, excitement, enthusiasm, caution, aggression, action, courage, success
Red	excitement, youthfulness, boldness, passion, activity, energy, leadership, will-power, confidence, ambition, power, hunger, love, appetite, urgency
Purple	creativity, imagination, wisdom, eccentricity, originality, individualism, wealth, modesty, compassion, eminence, respect, fantasy, royalty, success
Dark blue	trust, trustworthiness, strength, order, loyalty, sincerity, authority, communication, confidence, peace, integrity, control, responsibility, success, tranquility, masculinity, water, serenity, satiation, coldness, productivity, security

Light blue	spirituality, thoughtfulness, contentedness, control, help, determination, self-sufficiency, modernity, goals, awareness, purpose, accessibility, ambition
Green	peacefulness, growth, health, balance, restoration, equilibrium, positivity, nature, generosity, clarity, prosperity, good judgement, safety, stability, health, tranquility, money, growth, relaxation, wealth, fertility
Gray	balance, neutrality, tranquility
Pink	love, tranquility, respect, warmth, femininity, intuition, care, assertiveness, sensitivity, nurture, possibilities
Brown	friendliness, the earth, the outdoors, longevity, conservatism
Tan/beige	dependability, flexibility
Turquoise	spirituality, healing, protection, sophistication
Silver	glamor, technology, gracefulness, sleekness
Gold	wealth, prosperity, value, tradition
Black	protection, drama, class, formality
White	goodness, innocence, purity, freshness, ease, cleanliness

UNDERSTANDING VIDEO VIEWING HABITS

Attracting attention is an integral part of Facebook advertising. Your goal is to ensure your ad captures users' interest despite the competing content that surrounds it in News Feeds. The amount of attention you receive depends on your audience's viewing habits. There are three types of audiences: the audience that is on the go, that leans forward, and that leans back.

The On-the-Go Audience

People shuffling from home to work or traveling in trains, buses, or subways are considered an on-the-go audience, people who are traveling from point A to point B. Because these users quickly consume media content, they are the hardest people to stop mid-scroll. To attract their attention, make sure the first few seconds of your video are eye-catching. Additionally, make sure your main message appears within the first three seconds of your ad.

The Lean-Forward Audience

The lean-forward audience, unlike the on-the-go audience, is not traveling from point A to point B. Their attention is easier to capture, and they are more receptive to hearing your message. For this audience, try crafting videos that invite interaction, for example, encouraging viewers to voice their opinions in the comments section.

The Lean-Back Audience

A lean-back audience is composed of users whose attention is solely set on their mobile screens. These users are generally at home relaxing, and because this audience is the most receptive to your message, longer, immersive videos or live streams perform well.

AD ACCOUNT HISTORY

The history log is a useful feature that allows you to view the actions taken inside your Facebook ad account. These include the activity, activity details, item changed, changed by user, and date and time of the action.

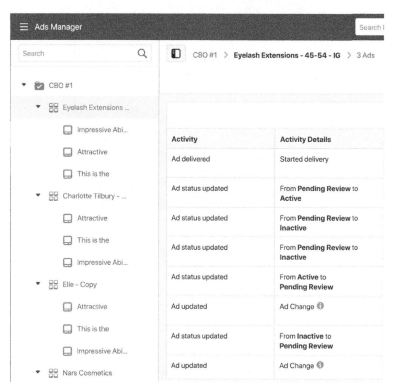

This can be very useful when it comes to monitoring billing or looking back on actions taken during key moments in your ad campaigns. For example, if all campaigns stopped delivering at midnight, you could look into your account history to see what actions happened during that time that might have caused the delivery issue. The history log also allows owners or managers to view the work completed by individuals working on the account. This is a critical tool for fact-checking claims about work being completed inside the account and who is actually completing the work.

To access your ad account history, follow these steps:

Step 1: Go to Ads Manager then Account Overview.

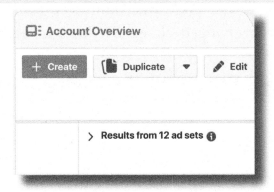

Step 2: Select the clock icon from the right side panel.

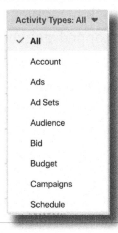

Step 3: Click **Activity Types > Account.**

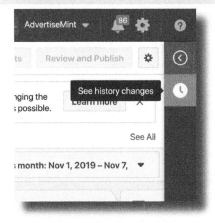

ANALYTICS

Custom Metrics in Ad Reports

Although Facebook's Ads Reporting page may seemingly contain all of the metrics you can possibly conceive of, you may find that one metric is missing. In this case, you will likely export the analytical report into a spreadsheet and manually create a formula for a new metric within a new column. With the Custom Metrics tool, you can skip this step and create your own metric inside Ads Reporting. To create a custom metric, you must go to the Ads Reporting page in Business Manager, click **Metrics** then **Create** under **Custom Metrics**.

When you fill in the information for your custom metrics, you will be asked to provide a metric description. This will define what the metric measures. For example, you can create a "reach" metric with description: "this metric measures the number of unique users reached." You will also be asked to provide a formula for how the metric is measured. For example, if you were creating a metric for cost per click, you would create this formula: amount spent ÷ link clicks = cost per click. Of course, the example metrics exist in Facebook's Ads Reporting page. Use Custom Metrics to create a metric that does not currently exist.

ACCOUNT

Delivery Issues

When you are experiencing delivery issues, it is best to check Delivery Insights, which you can access while viewing ad sets in Ads Manager. This tool shows you the problems with your ad's delivery. With this information, you can better diagnose delivery issues and improve results. The information in Delivery Insights also includes analyses explaining the reasons for delivery volatility and ways that you can address the problem.

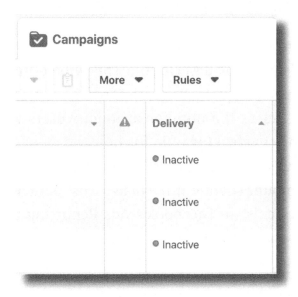

When accessing Delivery Insights, you will see three tabs that contain information about your ad set's performance:

Activity: This tab shows you the actions taken on a specific ad set, such as updates and deliveries.

Auction overlap: An auction overlap, one of the causes of your ad set's poor performance, occurs when you target an overlapping audience, causing you to bid against yourself. In this tab, you will gain access to information on other ad sets that overlap.

Audience saturation: This occurs when an audience sees your ads multiple times and refuses to respond to them. The audience saturation tab will provide information on audience saturation, such as the percentage of your daily impressions that comes from people seeing your ad set for the first time.

When your ad set experiences a performance shift, Facebook will send a notification that you can click to view. The notification will appear on the top-right corner of Ads Manager.

Only ad sets that have been running for at least five consecutive days, have at least 500 impressions, and have experienced a performance shift will have access to Delivery Insights.

THE LEARNING PHASE

For example, you are running sandals ads to everyone in the United States. As orders increase, Facebook will detect that most of the customers purchasing are from states where beaches are very popular, such as Hawaii, California and Florida. As a result, Facebook will show more ads to users in those areas. The learning phase is important because it allows Facebook to gather data needed to optimize for the best results.

The learning phase ends after 50 optimization events per ad set per week. Meaning, if you are running an ad with the app install objective, the learning phase ends after 50 app installs per ad set per week. If you turn your ads off before the 50 optimization events, Facebook will not have enough data for optimization, and the delivery will often slow or the CPMs will increase. Because the learning phase is integral to ad optimization, do not pause your ads too soon and do not make significant edits to your ads lest the learning phase restarts.

It is possible for the learning phase to end before the 50 optimization events. If your ad does not acquire 50 optimization events after enough time has passed, it is a sign that your ad is not performing well. In this case, you must edit your ad by changing the targeting or creative.

For the learning phase to continue without any delays or issues, you must have a large enough budget, depending on the number of ad sets you are running. Delays with the learning phase may arise if you are advertising an expensive item.

Once the learning phase ends you can make a data-led decision. If your ads are not performing well, turn them off. If they are performing well, scale. Because of the learning phase, you must let your ad run for a few more days to get better performance data. If you run your ads for two days and see unsatisfactory results, give it a few more days before killing the ads.

THE ATTRIBUTION WINDOW

The attribution window gives credit to your ad for purchases made from Facebook. The attribution window is the period of time between the click or view of your ad and the purchase of your product. For example, if a user clicked your ad and then purchased after 10 days, the attribution window is the 10 days that it took the user to convert. You can adjust that attribution to your preference, with options ranging from 1 day to 28 days, the default option.

There are two types of attribution windows: click window and view window. Click window is the period of time between when a user clicks on your ad and purchases your product. View window is the period of time between when a user views your ad and purchases a product. You can change your attribution windows for those two options in the settings of Business Manager. Click the tab ad accounts on the left menu, and you will find the attribution option on the right side of your screen. Slide the bar left to right to change your attribution windows.

Choose a longer attribution window for a cold audience or for an expensive product. Customers will usually deliberate before purchasing from you, especially if those customers are unfamiliar with your brand or planning to purchase an expensive product. Additionally, consider your clients' desires. Your clients prefer a seven-day attribution window or one-day attribution.

SCALING YOUR ADS

Facebook built its ad platform around momentum. In addition to your bid, Facebook monitors your ad's popularity, engagement, time, and completed objectives. If your ad has a large number of engagement and completed objectives, then it will perform well on the platform. However, like a hit song, your ads will not stay in the top position for long—every ad has a life cycle. Over time, your ad will underperform. This occurs because of ad fatigue: Users who have seen your ad too often will scroll past it because they no longer find it exciting. Once a new ad is launched, the clock on ad fatigue starts ticking.

It is critical that you do everything in your power to protect your momentum at the beginning and during the acceleration period. Ensure your ads accrue engagement (likes, reactions, comments, shares) by replying to every comment or running engagement campaigns. Avoid editing or duplicating your ads in the early stages, as that will restart the learning phase and slow your momentum. Use the ad's post ID when creating new versions to preserve its social proof.

Once you have all the elements of a hit ad, the next step is to scale your audience, bidding, and creatives.

WHEN TO SCALE

The prospect of growing your ad campaigns and, consequently, growing your returns, is an appealing one, so much so that you may approach this strategy with a little too much gusto. Reign that enthusiasm in because you cannot scale all of your ads. You can scale only those that are performing well. For example, if you are running an ad that converts at a high rate, scale immediately.

Before you scale your ad, however, let it run for a day or two. Doing so allows you to gather data that will tell you whether your ad is performing well. After you have gathered enough data, you can then decide whether you should scale. In some cases where the ad is generating mediocre results, it is better to allow the ad to run for a few more days before scaling. For example, your data revealed that your ad with the conversions objective generated a large number of engagement with little to no conversions. Evidently, your ad is underperforming. Although your engagement is high, which is a sign of user interest, the conversions, which are your ad's objective, are low. In this case, it would be unwise to scale the ad. Rather, run the ad for several more days to see if results improve. If not, pause your ad and refresh the creatives.

In other cases, it is best to stop your ad immediately. For example, if your ad has no conversions and has very little engagement, it is better to stop the ad before it spends more money. Identify the problem, whether it is your audience or your creative, and then create a solution.

HOW TO SCALE

There are a few ways to scale your ads.

Budget

When your ads perform well, increase your budget. Instead of making a significant budget increase, which often have a negative effect on ad performance, increase your budget by 10 to 15% on a daily basis. You can use the Automated Rules tool to increase your budget by a certain percentage every hour, day, or week, ensuring your ads continue their momentum.

Audience (Estimated Action Rates)

Increasing your audience will increase your estimated action rates, a core component of the Facebook auction, and your reach. You can scale your audience by expanding your Lookalike Audience size, adding more targeting options, targeting a wider demographic, or running ads in other countries. Although you can keep your successful campaigns and ad sets running, add new campaigns or ad sets into the mix.

Using campaign budget optimization with three to five ad sets containing large audiences will allow Facebook's algorithm to look through those audiences, find the best-performing segments, and focus your budget in those segments. In addition to this strategy, you can also create a campaign with 50 different ad sets, each set containing one targeting element. You can reach users at a much lower cost by including unpopular targeting options. Additional strategies include duplicating the best campaigns and running both inside the same ad account; and creating a secondary ad account, sharing the pixel, and running your best ads inside the account to ensure they are reaching more people.

Bidding

Your bid is the biggest factor in winning the auction and ensuring your ad appears to Facebook users. Remember: To win the auction, you will pay more than the next closest bid. For example, if advertiser A bids

$500 and advertiser B bids $25, advertiser A will most likely pay $26 for the ad to appear first.

To ensure your ads are delivered more often, increase your bid. Facebook recommends placing your true bid, the amount you make from the sale. For example, if advertiser A sells a product for $500, which costs $100 to produce and market, Facebook would recommend bidding $400. Although you will not likely pay $400 to display an ad, that amount will win the auction. A common tactic is to bid well beyond your true bid, which helps your ad quickly generate more impressions. However, be sure to monitor your ads, as this change in the auction can quickly affect your results.

Ad Creatives

One of the best ways to improve performance and scale is to upload new creatives. A rule of thumb: Never show the same ad to the same person more than twice. This is extremely difficult to do when you have a higher budget. Use Dynamic Creatives or create a schedule for new ad releases every few days. You are paying to get in front of users' eyes—it is better to show your potential customers new and exciting ads rather than a rerun.

ADVANCED PIXEL OPTIONS

There are many advanced options that are available with the Facebook pixel. These often require additional coding or development, but they can add significant value to the data you are collecting. Facebook has provided instructions for how to implement the following:

- Installing the pixel using an IMG tag

- Tracking clicks on buttons

- Triggering events based on visibility

- Triggering events based on page length or percentage

- Delayed pixel fires

- Triggering events based on articles viewed per session

- Selective event tracking with multiple pixels

- Tracking events for individual pixels

- Automatic configuration

Visit the following page to see detailed instructions for setting up each action:

https://developers.facebook.com/docs/facebook-pixel/advanced/

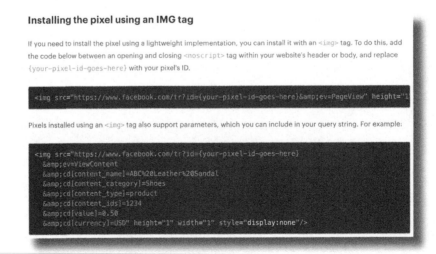

CHAPTER 9: RESTRICTED ADVERTISING CATEGORIES

POLITICAL ADVERTISING

If you are running political, election, or social issues ads on Facebook, you must be authorized to run those types of ads. To prevent misuse, Facebook will require you to verify your ID and finish the authorization process. Only advertisers from certain countries can apply for authorization. To see the list of countries that are eligible, visit the Facebook Business website:

https://www.facebook.com/business/help/208949576550051

Advertisers in the United States must have all of the items in the authorization checklist to qualify:

- A Facebook page of which you are an admin

- Two-factor authentication enabled on Facebook account

- Driver's license, state ID, or passport

All of your political, social issues, and election ads will appear on users' feeds with the "Paid for by" disclaimer. Without the disclaimer, the ads will not be approved to run. Those ads will also appear in the Ad Library, under the Ad Library Report section, where the public can access all of your paused and active ads, as well as the ad targeting, disclaimers, and total spend for each. The Ad Library exists to provide greater transparency, a goal that has become a bigger priority since the Cambridge Analytica scandal and the proliferation of fake Russian ads in 2016.

To visit the Ad Library Report, use the following URL:

https://www.facebook.com/ads/library/report

GETTING AUTHORIZATION FOR POLITICAL ADS

To apply for authorization to run political, social issues, and election ads, you must follow these steps:

> Step 1: Go to your Facebook page, then click **Settings > Authorizations.**

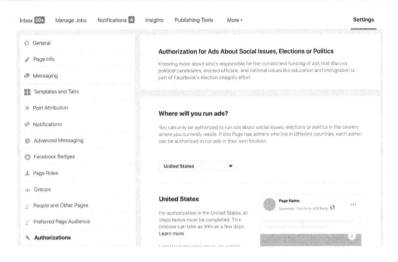

> Step 2: Select your country, confirm your identity, set up your primary location, provide identification, answer screening questions, then click **Finish**.

After you send your information, Facebook will mail your confirmation code to the mailing address you provided during the authorization process. The letter with the code will take approximately three to seven days to arrive if you are in the United States. To check the status of your letter, go to the Authorizations page again and click **View** next to your name.

If your letter does not arrive, you can request a new one using this URL:

https://www.facebook.com/id

REAL ESTATE, EMPLOYMENT, AND CREDIT ADS

To ensure all real estate ads follow all applicable laws and do not discriminate, Facebook launched the Special Ad Audience. This ad-targeting option prevents discriminatory advertising practices by providing behavioral targeting options rather than options related to personal attributes. For example, with Special Ad Audience, you can no longer target a group based on their multicultural affinities, age, gender, and ZIP code. This option appears at the Campaign level and must be selected if you are running housing, employment, or credit ads. Ads submitted will be evaluated by automatic and human reviews to ensure that they do not violate applicable laws. The following ad targeting options will not be available: ZIP code, age, gender, and certain detailed targeting options.

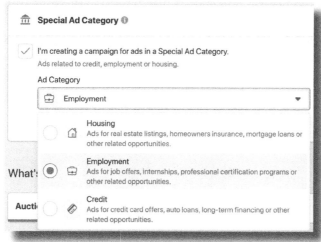

To run real estate, employment, and credit ads, you must click the **Special Ad Category** option in the campaign level of Ads Manager. If you do not do this, your ads will not run. When you run an ad under the Special Ad Category, you will not be able to use Lookalike Audiences. Instead, you will use the Special Ad Audience, which searches for users similar to your current audience without using personal attributes as a targeting criteria. You also will not be able to use a previously saved audience. You must create a new audience source.

CRYPTOCURRENCY

Facebook banned cryptocurrency ads from its platform but later changed the policy to be more lenient. Now Facebook allows approved advertisers to run ads that promote cryptocurrency. When applying to be an approved advertiser, you must provide the following information:

- You Facebook ad account ID

- The website domain related to your ad account

- Documents related to your business, such as press releases

- Business information, including name and address

To apply, visit Facebook's Contact page:

https://www.facebook.com/help/contact/532535307141067

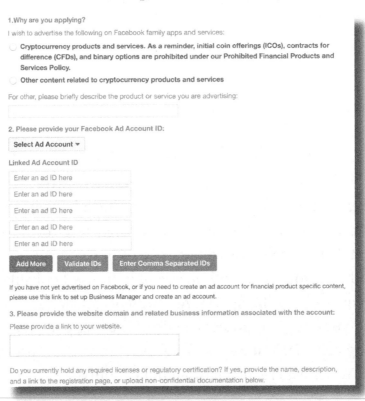

CHAPTER 10: FACEBOOK BLUEPRINT

Thanks to its self-serve platform, Facebook advertising makes it easy for anyone to create ads and advertise. Unfortunately, opening advertising to everyone comes with drawbacks. Even people who are not highly skilled can dabble and experiment on Facebook. For this reason, Facebook launched Blueprint Certification in September 2016 to establish credibility in the industry and to set a standard for media-buying on its platform. Blueprint Certification is a credential that proves you are a skilled and qualified Facebook advertiser. Think of it as your diploma from college that proves you are trained and qualified for the field you studied.

CERTIFICATIONS

To obtain certification, you must take a 90-minute Blueprint test. One test will give you one certification. If you fail, you must wait five days and pay the fees again to retake the test.

Facebook Certified Digital Marketing Associate: For entry-level Facebook advertisers, the test will ask beginner-level questions. For example, it will require you to identify the difference between a post and an ad, name Facebook's family of apps, and describe the steps in creating an ad account.

Facebook Certified Media Planning Professional: This test is recommended for media and digital planners. The test covers brand awareness, brand and conversion lift studies, and reach and frequency.

Facebook Certified Media Buying Planning: This test, geared for advanced marketers, will ask questions, such as reach and frequency, how Ads Manager works, the different strategies used to optimize for clients' goals, and brand awareness.

Facebook Certified Product Developer I: This test will cover topics about the technical aspects of Facebook advertising, for example, how to install the Facebook Pixel, create product catalogs, and set up standard events and custom conversions.

Facebook Certified Product Developer II: This test is recommended for app and website developers with coding experience. It will ask questions about the SDK, app events, Dynamic Ads, and offline conversions. Be ready to finish coding exercises.

Facebook Certified Product Developer III: Also recommended for app and website developers, this test will focus on configuring issues with API integrations. Writing code and setting up infrastructure will be the main topic of the test.

To access study materials for each test, visit the Facebook Business website:

https://www.facebook.com/business/learn/certification

CHAPTER 11: FACEBOOK ADS RESOURCES

RESOURCES FOR ADVERTISERS

Advertiser Support: For issues regarding your ads, billing, getting started with Facebook advertising, pages, and permissions.

https://www.facebook.com/business/resources

Facebook Technical Services: Become a partner for technical services and appear in Facebook's Partner Category. To be eligible, you must have the Facebook Certified Ads Product Developer Certification.

https://www.facebook.com/business/m/fmp-technical-services

Facebook Learn: Blueprint courses for learning how to advertise on Facebook and taking the Blueprint Certification test.

https://www.facebook.com/business/learn

Facebook Blueprint: The website where you can register for Blueprint exams.

https://www.facebook.com/business/learn/certification

Facebook Business Videos: Informative and instructional videos about Facebook advertising include talks at Cannes Lions and DMEXCO, and advice on how to succeed on Facebook.

https://www.facebook.com/pg/facebookbusiness/videos/

Agency Hub: Contains support for advertising agencies. Here you can contact customer support and Blueprint resources, and sign up for agency events.

https://www.facebook.com/business/m/fmp/agencies

Facebook Ads Manager: A mobile-app version of Ads Manager so you can manage and create ads from your phone.

iPhone:
https://apps.apple.com/us/app/facebook-ads-manager/id964397083

Android:
https://play.google.com/store/apps/details?id=com.facebook.adsmanager

Facebook Events: Find upcoming events and access recaps of events you missed.

https://www.facebook.com/business/events

Facebook IQ Insights: Contains articles about the studies Facebook commissions. A good resource for finding statistics on Facebook's users and trends on the platform.

https://www.facebook.com/business/news/insights

Facebook Ad Formats Guide: Resources on how to create certain ad formats and guides on ad specs.

https://www.facebook.com/business/ads-guide

Curated by Facebook: Get featured on Facebook's social media by submitting your story. For artists, agency or brand representatives, and production companies.

https://www.facebook.com/curatedbyfb

Facebook Developers: Contains updates on VR, F8, resources about apps, and a tab to access your apps linked to Facebook.

https://developers.facebook.com/

Good Questions. Real Answers: A new section in Facebook Business where people can read answers to common advertising questions. Those answers, provided by Facebook's employees, address issues related to data and privacy, ad policies, safety, and measurement.

https://www.facebook.com/business/good-questions

Pending Facebook Ads Issues: Contains a form that allows you to submit a case about ads that have been pending for more than 24 hours.

https://www.facebook.com/help/contact/515460121837726/

App Ads Helper: Troubleshoots and fixes any problems with your app. There are various app management actions you can do with this tool: verify your app, check your app's settings, install events, and view your app's history, installs, and bid type.

https://developers.facebook.com/tools/app-ads-helper/

Facebook Groups: Join a community of like-minded Facebook advertisers to discuss strategy, tips, and resources.

https://www.facebook.com/groups/advertisemint/

Ads Status Page: Alerts you of any outages to the platform that may disrupt your ability to create, launch, or manage ads in Ads Manager.

status.fb.com/ads

FACEBOOK ADVERTISING EVENTS

F8: The three-day Facebook for Developers conference covers product launches, VR, and updates to Facebook, Messenger, WhatsApp, and Instagram.

https://www.f8.com/

Social Media Marketing World: Based in San Diego, California, this conference welcomes influencers and marketers to discuss tactics in social media marketing.

https://www.socialmediaexaminer.com/smmworld/

Traffic and Conversion Summit: This San Diego-based event was created for marketing professionals, agency owners, consultants, and entrepreneurs to share the latest strategies on digital marketing.

https://trafficandconversionsummit.com

ManyChat Conversations Conference: Connect with industry leaders, learn about messenger marketing and strategies, and network with professionals from various industries.

https://conversationsconference.com/about/

RESOURCES FOR YOUR CREATIVE TEAM

Video Creation Kit: Learn about Facebook's video creation kit, which helps create lightweight videos made of still images.

https://www.facebook.com/business/news/making-it-easier-to-build-mobile-first-video-ads

Facebook Spark AR Studio: Create filters for Instagram and Facebook Stories.

https://sparkar.facebook.com/ar-studio/

Facebook Creative Shop: Ad examples with information on placement and option to create mockups.

https://www.facebook.com/business/inspiration

Creative Apps

Photoshop Express: https://www.photoshop.com/products/photoshopexpress

Adobe Spark Post: https://spark.adobe.com/

PicLab: https://play.google.com/store/apps/details?id=com.apperto.piclabapp&hl=en_US

Ripl: https://www.ripl.com/

VideoShop: https://www.videoshop.net/

Quik: https://gopro.com/en/us/shop/softwareandapp/quik-%7C-desktop/Quik-Desktop.html

Boomerang: https://apps.apple.com/us/app/boomerang-from-instagram/id1041596399

Legend: https://play.google.com/store/apps/details?id=com.animate.legend&hl=en_US

VlogEasy: https://vlogeasy.com/

CHAPTER 12: INSTAGRAM ADVERTISING

Instagram is one of the world's most popular social media apps. With so many users frequenting the app, it is easy to imagine finding the right customer for your business on the platform. More than 200 million Instagrammers visit at least one business profile a day. There are two ways you can advertise on Instagram: through Ads Manager and with boosted posts on the Instagram app.

INSTAGRAM AD OPTIONS

You can use most of the objectives offered in Ads Manager for your Instagram ads, which appear in three areas of the app: in Stories, the feed, and the Explore page.

Stories: Ads will be in the 9:16 ratio as either a video or a photo that will appear for a maximum of 15 seconds between users' Stories. Users can either swipe up on your CTA button, click back to rewatch your story, click forward to skip it, or exit out of Stories. If they click on your ad, your landing page will load within the app.

Feed: Ads, either as a video or single image, will appear in the feeds of users, among the posts of the accounts they follow. Once clicked, the ads will open your chosen landing page within the app.

Explore: Ads appearing in the Instagram Explore area will appear if users click on a post and scroll to see more content. The ad will appear among the posts users are scrolling through.

INSTAGRAM ADS VIA ADS MANAGER

You have two options for creating an Instagram ad. You can either boost a post from your profile or create the ad in Ads Manager. Many advertisers use the latter method. To ensure your Instagram ads appear on the app, you must have the following:

Instagram Business Profile: Without an Instagram business profile, you cannot advertise on the app.

Instagram Connected to Business Manager: If you do not connect your Instagram account to Business Manager, you will not be able to run ads on Instagram. You can add Instagram accounts in the Business Settings page.

Select Instagram as Placement: Although choosing automatic placements will serve your ads to Instagram, if you want your ads to appear only on that app, make sure to select Instagram when editing placement options.

Select Instagram as Identity: If you do not choose Instagram as your identity, when the ads run on Instagram, users will not be able to visit your profile when they click on your account name or default picture.

INSTAGRAM ADS VIA THE INSTAGRAM APP

In order to run ads through the Instagram app, you will need to set up three accounts. It is recommended that you have a Business Manager account before attempting to run Instagram ads. You must also have a business page and an Instagram business account. You do not need to create a new profile to get a business account. You can simply switch from your regular account to a business account from your Settings: Go to **Settings > Account > Switch to Professional Account.**

When advertising ads from the Instagram app, you will be able to promote only organic content that you posted. The organic post will be converted into an ad, appearing to both Instagram feeds and Stories. After you publish an image or video, a **Promote** button will appear on the bottom-right corner of your posts. When you click it, the page for creating an ad will appear.

CREATING INSTAGRAM ADS FROM THE APP

Then you must click your ad, your target audience, and your budget before selecting the landing page where users will be redirected.

Where to Send People: Your options will include sending traffic directly to your profile, to your website or landing page, or into Direct, Instagram's messaging feature. Each option will come with an accompanying CTA button. For example, the profile option generates a **Visit Instagram Profile** CTA button, which directs users to your profile to view more content. The website option will send users to your website or landing page. The direct message option, which includes a **Send Message** CTA button, will prompt users to send you a direct message. There are numerous other CTAs to choose from, including buttons that urge users to "Learn More," "Shop Now," "Watch More," "Contact Us," "Book Now," and "Sign Up."

Select the Audience: Instagram provides two options for ad targeting. The first is Automatic Targeting, which selects the users Instagram believes will most likely complete your desired action. The second is manual targeting. This option allows you to select the location, interests, age, and gender of your target audience. You can then name the audience and save it for later.

Select Budget and Duration: You can select a budget between $1 and $1,000 a day, along with your duration, which is between 1 and 30 days.

If you are creating ads on Instagram for the first time, you will need to enter your billing information before you can submit the ads for approval. Once they are submitted, the ads will be reviewed and, if approved, will begin running within a few hours.

PROMOTED POST INSIGHTS

Once your ads run, you will be able to view the status by visiting the original post and clicking **View Insights**. There you can see data on your ads' URL clicks, comments, saves, and likes. You can view the information for all ads by clicking the **Promotions** button on your profile, or by visiting **Menu Bar > Settings > Ads > Ads Activity**.

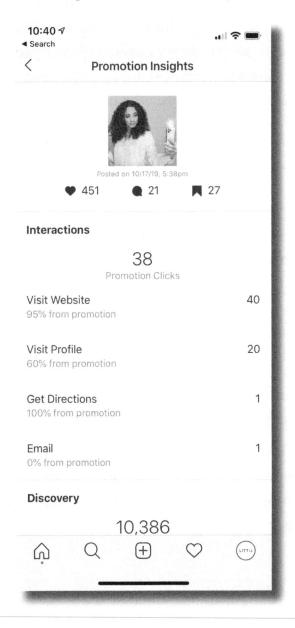

BRANDED CONTENT ADS

With Branded Content Ads, you can create ads using the organic posts of influencers promoting your products or services. You can find those posts within Ads Manager under Existing Posts. To enable Branded Content Ads, approve content from creators, and run ads, you must follow the required steps:

In the Instagram app, go to **Settings > Business > Branded Content > Enable Require Approvals**. Click **Approved Accounts** and select your brand partner's Instagram account. This will allow that account to tag you on branded content. This can also be done through Ads Manager at the Ad Level by clicking **Use Existing Post,** then **Select Post** and choosing the branded post that you want to promote on Instagram.

BILLING

For billing issues, you can update your billing or select your ad account in the Instagram app by going to **Settings > Business > Promotion Payments**. From there you can select the Facebook account you want associated or update the card on file.

To enable Instagram Shopping, visit **Settings > Business > Shopping**. This option allows you to tag posts with products that appear in your attached catalogs so visitors can link right to the product page to purchase. You will need to have a catalog enabled in Business Manager. Once that is completed, you will be able to select it and submit for review. Once approved, the post should appear in your account within a few days.

CHAPTER 13: MESSENGER MARKETING

Before chatbots, customers primarily communicated with businesses through phone calls and emails. However, as technology advanced and smartphones became even smarter phones, customers have moved away from email and phone calls to messaging. As of Q2 2019, Facebook Messenger and WhatsApp have an estimated 2.1 billion users accessing the apps every day on average, and a study commissioned by Facebook found that messaging apps are predicted to have a 23% increase in usage. Messenger marketing is increasing in importance, and every business owner must adapt to this shift in trends.

HOW IT WORKS

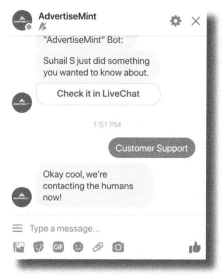

Messenger marketing allows you to increase the subscribers of your messenger apps, such as Facebook Messenger or ManyChat. Once your customers are subscribed, you can send them marketing messages, such as an alert about a product sale, a blog post, or a prompt to sign up for an email newsletter. You can also talk to customers through live chat, and if none of your customer service representatives are at the computer when a message arrives, you can set up automated responses using the bot program of your choice.

GENERATE LEADS WITH MESSENGER

Using a Clicks to Messenger Ad, you can nurture your leads straight from the Facebook Messenger app. With the roll-out of lead generation in Messenger, you can create an ad that brings customers to your Messenger conversation. Once there they can answer the question that appears, using the options given in front of their screens. You can integrate with your CRM provider and continue your conversation in the inbox of your Facebook page, the Ads Manager App, or a third-party live-chat software, such as Salesforce or LiveChat.

To generate leads within Messenger, follow these steps:

Step 1: In Ads Manager, create a campaign with the **Messages** objective.

Step 2: In the ad set level under the **Messenger Destination**, choose **Click to Messenger**.

Step 3: In the ad level under **Messenger Setup**, click **Generate Leads** then **Create Chat**.

Step 4: Fill in the fields.

Step 5: Submit your ad for review.

When filling in the required fields, make sure the greeting you create references the message in the ad. It is best to start with multiple-choice questions and end with actionable next steps. Prompt customers to visit your website and provide a link.

TECHNOLOGY PARTNER: MANYCHAT

ManyChat is the leading chatbot-building tool that helps you automate Facebook Messenger responses to customers' requests, comments, and queries. ManyChat is free to use, and you can use ManyChat to achieve several different business goals. For example, you can use it to direct traffic to your website, increase sales by sending discount codes to subscribers, or acquire subscribers by creating a Messenger ad that, once clicked, automatically adds users to your list.

When you log in to your ManyChat account, you will notice the tabs in the left column of your page. There you will find the tabs dashboard, audience, live chat, growth tools, and broadcasting.

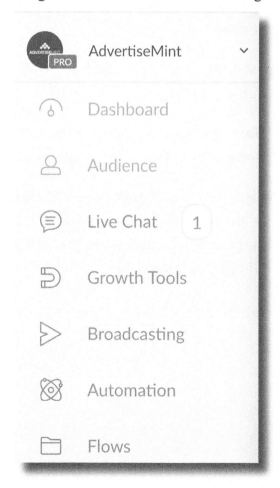

- **Dashboard:** Contains information about your account, such as number of subscribes, unsubscribes, and net subscribers.

- **Audience:** Contains your list of subscribers. Here you can search for subscribers, remove subscribers, find more information about subscribers, add or remove a tag for subscribers, and move subscribers in different sequences.

- **Live Chat:** Contains the non-automated conversations you have with your customers. If you want to speak directly to your customers, you can do so here.

- **Growth Tools:** Contains overlays, pop-ups, and widgets you can create for your website to encourage people to message you on Facebook Messenger.

- **Broadcasting:** Allows you to schedule and send broadcast messages to your subscribers.

- **Automation:** Here you can create messages that your bot will automatically send to people who message you.

- **Flows:** A flow is a process a user goes through. It can contain many different outcomes based on what the user inputs into Messenger. Flows can contain text, images, videos, galleries, lists, audio, video, files or dynamic fields.

CREATE A MESSENGER BOT WITH MANYCHAT

Bots can be very powerful and complex. Building a bot involves creating a welcome message, keywords, and flows.

WELCOME MESSAGE

The first step is to create a welcome message, the automatic response customers will receive once they contact you on Facebook Messenger. The automatic message should contain a question with several actionable steps customers can select. Basic bots provide pre-selected answers while advanced bots process keywords and provide custom answers based on the words that users enter. To create a welcome message, go to Automation > Welcome Message.

KEYWORDS

Keywords trigger responses from bots. Examples of common keywords include "help," "customer support," "sign up," and "unsubscribe." If you expect users to enter any of these words when communicating with your bot, you should create automated responses for those keywords to ensure users receive a message that is relevant to their needs.

To create keywords, go to Automation > Keywords. Click New Keyword. Enter your keywords and choose the desired action you want to happen. You can add a tag, subscribe customers to your bot, notify admins, or even add them to a custom audience.

BUILDING A FLOW

Flows are the automated conversation you want users to go through. The flows can be simple and contain plain text or complex and contain images, gifs, videos, galleries, lists, audio, video, files, or dynamic content based on users' input. Flows, when mapped out, appear as a sideways tree, with one greeting branching out into several possible responses.

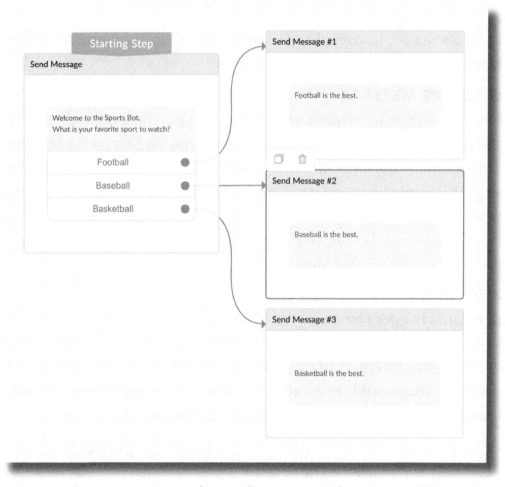

To create a flow, go to **Manychat > Flow > New Flow**. You will be asked to add a starting step and select what happens at each of the next steps. This can continue on as you build your desired conversation. Flows can be improved over time as you see areas where people may be stuck or have a question that you are failing to offer as a selection. As users enter responses, you can tag the user and sync the responses with Google Spreadsheets or your marketing CRM to ensure all your customer information is up to date.

LINKING A FLOW TO YOUR FACEBOOK AD

You can run Messenger ads that are linked to your ManyChat bot.

Step 1: On Manychat, click on **Growth Tools > Create New Growth Tool > Facebook Ads JSON**

Step 2: Click on the setup link and copy your JSON code.

Step 3: Create your ad campaign and select **Messages** as the objective.

Step 4: On the ad level, visit **Messenger Setup > Create New > Advanced JSON Setup**. Click the edit button.

Paste your ManyChat JSON code, and your Facebook ad will link directly to your growth tool. You will need to add a welcome message and link the first step to your flow.

CHAPTER 14: FACEBOOK PAGE TOOLS

To maintain a business presence on Facebook, you must update your Facebook page and enable certain features to improve the experience of your page visitors and followers. This is especially important because your page will represent all of the ads that appear on Facebook's platforms. When users click on your profile to visit your page, you must ensure that the page they see is in its best shape. There are several managing tools you can use to maintain your Facebook page.

ASSIGNING PAGE ROLES

Managing a page alone can be difficult, especially if your page receives a constant flow of comments and messages from hundreds of followers. Fortunately, you can assign page roles such as editor, advertiser, admin, and analyst to your team, who can help you manage your page.

Step 1: Go to your Facebook page > **Settings** > **Page Roles**.

Step 2: Add members, assign page roles, edit page roles, or remove members.

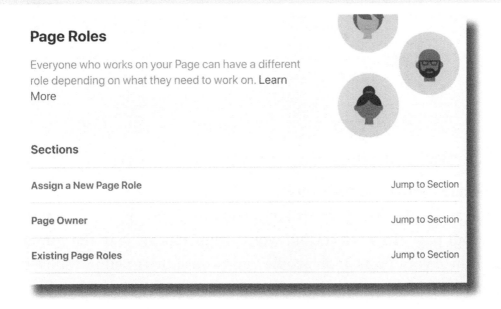

Page Roles

Everyone who works on your Page can have a different role depending on what they need to work on. **Learn More**

Sections

Assign a New Page Role	Jump to Section
Page Owner	Jump to Section
Existing Page Roles	Jump to Section

ADDING AN INSTAGRAM ACCOUNT

If you want to create Instagram ads without connecting your Instagram account to Business Manager, add your Instagram account to your Facebook page.

Step 1: Go to your Facebook page > **Settings** > **Instagram** > **Connect Account.**

Step 2: Follow the steps to connect your Instagram account.

Blocking Words and Profanity

You can block certain words and profanity from appearing anywhere on your page. To block certain words from appearing in the comments section of your posts or on people's posts on your Timeline, follow these steps:

Blocking Words

Step 1: Click **General > Page Moderation**.

Step 2: Enter words to block. Save changes.

Filtering Profanity

Step 1: Click **Profanity Filter**. Choose degree. Save.

Filtering profanity works differently than blocking words. While you choose the words you want to block, Facebook determines which profane language to block based on commonly reported words and phrases marked as offensive by the community. It also blocks profanity according to the degree you choose. Choosing medium will block moderately vulgar profanity, while choosing strong will block only strongly vulgar profanity.

Verifying Your Facebook Page

If you own a Facebook page categorized under a local business, company, or organization, then your page is eligible for a gray verification badge. Verification badges let your page visitors know that your page is authentic. While blue verification badges are for public figures, celebrities, and brands, gray verification badges are for businesses and companies.

Step 1: Go to **Settings > General > Page Verification**.

Step 2: Choose to verify with either a phone number or a document. Fill in the required information.

ADDING A CTA BUTTON TO YOUR PAGE

CTA buttons are a great way to encourage followers and page visitors to take a desired action. CTA buttons can encourage them to shop at your online store, book an appointment, learn more about your business, or sign up for email notifications. With CTA buttons, you can easily and quickly connect with a potential customer.

Step 1: Click **Add a Button** on the lower-right corner of your cover photo.

Step 2: Follow the instructions on the screen.

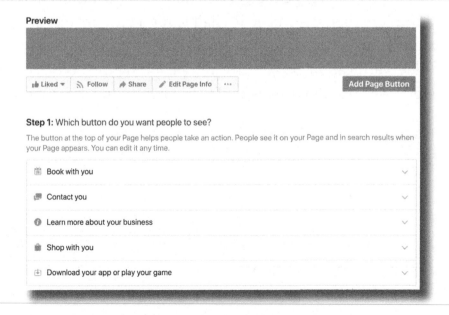

UNDERSTANDING FACEBOOK ANALYTICS

Facebook Analytics is a free tool included in Business Manager that contains a trove of information about people's interaction with your business across your website, Facebook page, Messenger, and app. Facebook Analytics acquires customer information from four channels: your website, apps, Facebook page, and Messenger.

Analytics Channels

Website contains information about website activity, such as the actions and demographics of your web visitors. It also contains features that allow you to create funnels to measure conversion, see demographics and segments to learn about your web visitors, and measure behaviors over time.

Apps contains aggregated demographics and information about the people who use your app; for example, information about the number of users who open your app and the number of times users purchase inside your app.

Facebook Page contains information about your Facebook page visitors: their demographics, their dates and times of visit, their locations, and more.

Messenger contains information about interactions between you and your customers on Facebook Messenger.

ANALYTICS OVERVIEW

The overview is the first page you will see upon entering Facebook Analytics. There you will see categories for information separated by boxes that you can click for more details.

Key Metrics contains the metrics most likely to be important to you. You will see the numbers for unique users, new users, active conversations, and new conversations.

People contains the demographics of your most active visitors. The information includes the age, gender, and country of your visitors. Use this information to know your customers. This information may be useful for your ad targeting.

Other than viewing the metrics for your Facebook page or website, you can also use the tools Facebook Analytics offers.

Funnels is a tool that contains all the funnels you created to map your website visitors' customer journeys.

User Retention shows you how users are retaining information about your product or brand over time. This is the tool to use.

Cohorts shows the cohorts, or the groups of users who perform two events of your choosing over time.

Journeys shows your customers' interactions with your different channels. This tool contains the following metrics:

Events contains all of your pre-defined and custom events, or actions that people take in your channels. Along with events, the tool also contains event metrics, such as count, unique users, value, and description.

Event Debugging checks whether your events are logging correctly.

Lifetime Value contains the data of your lifetime value chart.

CHAPTER 15: HIRING AD MANAGEMENT

Facebook advertising is tricky. It is now a team sport that requires media buyers, video editors, graphic designers, copywriters, bot builders, and social media managers to run a truly effect campaign. If you want to improve the results for your Facebook advertising campaigns, you have a few options.

AGENCIES

Agencies have highly skilled individuals who manage Facebook advertising on clients' behalf. Companies often hire an agency if they are busy or if their ad budget is more than $5,000 a month. There are a few elements you should keep in mind when it comes to agencies.

Facebook Blueprint Certification
Anyone managing a company's ad budget should be Facebook Blueprint-certified. There are many agencies that claim to be experts but instead learn on the job. Because novices experiment with the client's money, it is important that anyone managing ads has Blueprint Certification.

Facebook Marketing Partners
Facebook has an agency program in which agencies are paired with Facebook marketing representatives who deliver solutions to advertising campaigns. The program is not open to everyone, and the level of service depends on the agency's managed ad spend. Facebook ranks agencies on three levels: premium, preferred, and account.

Account: $1,500 in monthly ad spend managed

Preferred: $500,000 in monthly ad spend managed

Premium: $5,000,000 in monthly ad spend managed

The agencies with more ad spend receive more benefits and a higher level of attention than the agencies with lower ad spend. When working with an agency, companies often have the expertise of both the account managers and the Facebook marketing partners.

Team

An agency brings an entire team to help ensure all critical elements are managed at a fraction of the cost of hiring employees. All companies that plan to hire an agency must ask which tasks are managed by which team members.

Office vs Remote

If you are working with an agency, it is wise to clarify if the agency's employees are working under the same roof or remotely. This will set expectations and avoid any issues with remote-based teams.

Freelancers

Hiring a freelancer is a great option if your monthly ad budget is lower than $5,000. Whether or not you should hire freelancers to manage your ad accounts depends on your preference. Although there are certainly benefits to hiring freelancers, there are also drawbacks.

Hiring freelancers is easier now more than ever, made possible by the existence of websites that connect employers with people searching for freelance work, websites such as Upwork, Freelancer.com, and Thumbtack. Hire a freelancer if you have a limited budget. With a freelancer, you can cut costs in areas such as insurance, office supplies, and office space. Additionally, you pay freelancers only when a job is completed. However, there are a few reasons that you may not want to hire a freelance account manager. If you prefer to supervise your employees, then a freelancer is not the right option for you. Because freelancers are often not in office and complete work remotely, it will be hard to determine whether or not the freelancer is doing the assigned job. Additionally, freelancers often take on multiple clients at once, so it is possible that those freelancers are not as invested in your company as an in-house employee.

In-House Account Manager

An in-house account manager is an individual who works in the office at your company. If you do not want to pay an agency price, but you do want an account manager who is available at all times and whom you can monitor in person, then an in-house account manager may be the right choice for you.

The benefit of hiring someone in-house is twofold. One, you can closely monitor your employee and ask for updates without the need to arrange a phone call or a meeting. Two, you know exactly who you are hiring and what to expect, since your hiring department carefully screened and chose the employee. However, with an in-house employee, you may not receive the benefits that come with an agency, for example, multiple Facebook Blueprint-certified account managers who will monitor your account and a partnership with Facebook's marketing representatives.

Self-Managed Ads

Managing your own campaigns is usually the most cost-effective method for running and profiting off ads. It is especially beneficial if you prefer to be hands-on with your campaigns and learn what ad and content perform best for your business. The disadvantage is time. As Facebook continues to roll out new features, the ad platform becomes more complex and time-intensive. There is more data to dig through and more campaigns to monitor. Very few Facebook campaigns can be left to run without monitoring and maintenance. Managing your own ads works well for start-up and small-business owners who want to get started with Facebook ads with a limited budget.

CHAPTER 16: FACEBOOK AND INSTAGRAM USER TOOLS

After Cambridge Analytica, Facebook users wanted to know more about the ways the company uses their data. In particular, people wanted to know whether or not Facebook sells their information to advertisers or listens to their conversations from their phones. As a result, Facebook created the following transparency tools that help users easily access their data, behavioral information, and content, and control how the social media company uses it:

Timeline Review: Tagged posts by users not in your friends list appear here. You can find Timeline Review by clicking the **Activity Log** button located on the lower-right corner of your cover photo.

News Feed Preferences: Here you can change you who want to see first on your News Feed, as well as manage your unfollow and snooze settings. You can access this feature by clicking the upside-down button on the upper-right corner of your desktop screen or the Settings page under News Feed Settings in your app.

View Your Ad Preferences: Here you can review how Facebook uses your data as ad targeting. You will find information about the ads you liked and the advertisers who used your information for ad targeting. You can also control which personal information you can prevent advertisers from using. You can find your ad preferences in the Settings page of your app (under View Your Ad Preferences) and desktop device (under Ads).

Download Your Facebook Data: The information you can download includes messages you received, content you engaged with, your search history, and the advertisers who used your information for ad targeting. You can access this tool from your desktop device under **Settings > Your**

Facebook Information or your app under **Settings > Download Your Information**.

Off-Facebook Activity: Here you can review your off-Facebook activity, such as using your Facebook login to access apps or visiting a website, and disconnect the information from your account to prevent the social media company from using your offline behavior for ad targeting. You can find this tool under **Settings > Your Off Facebook Activity**.

Facebook Clear History Tool: This tool allows you to clear or disassociate your off-Facebook data from your account. You can find this tool under **Settings > Your Off Facebook Activity > Clear History**.

Instagram Data and History Tool: This tool allows you to access all the personal and activity data that Instagram has about you, then download this data. You can also view any apps or third parties that you have enabled for Instagram and clear your search history on Instagram. You can find this tool inside the **Instagram App > Settings > Security > Data and History**.

CHAPTER 17: ANALYZING RESULTS

After you publish your Facebook ads, you must analyze your results. You can view all of your results in Ads Manager by clicking on a campaign. Once you click on a campaign, you will see columns with metrics such as reach, frequency, cost per results, and budget. Those are the columns you should look at when you want to view your analytical data. If you ran boosted posts from Instagram, you will find your analytics in Instagram's app.

Ads Manager Analytics

CTR (Link Click-Through): Your CTR, or click-through rate, is the number of clicks on your ad's link that takes users to a URL destination; for example, a page on your website. You can use this percentage to determine whether your ad is relevant to your audience. A low CTR may indicate that your ad is not attracting your audience's attention.

CPC (Cost per Link Click): CPC is the average cost for each link click. If your CPC is at $1.25, you are paying $1.25 each time a user clicks on your ad. You can calculate CPC by dividing the total amount spent on your ad by link clicks.

Impressions: The number of times your ads appear on users' screens. If a user, scrolling down News Feed, came upon your ad, Facebook would count that instance as one impression. If that user scrolled back up to see the ad, that still counts as one impression because the impression came from the same user.

CPM (Cost per 1,000 Impressions): CPM is the average cost for 1,000 impressions. It is calculated by dividing the total amount spent by impressions and multiplying by 1,000.

Cost per Result: Your cost per result is the average cost per outcome based on the objective you chose for your ad. For example, if your objective is conversions, then your result is purchases. Cost per result is calculated by dividing the amount you spent by the number of results you gained.

Frequency: The number of times you saw that ad on your feed is called frequency.

Reach: The number of people who saw your ad at least once.

Relevance Score: A rating from 1 to 10, relevance score determines whether your ads will be shown to your target audience in comparison to your competitors'. If your relevance score is low, Facebook will not show your ad to your audience as often because the company believes the ad will not resonate with the people you are targeting. Make sure your relevance score is 7 or above.

Website Purchase ROAS (Return on Ad Spend): The website purchase ROAS shows you how much money you make per dollar spent.

Cost per Website Purchase: The average cost of your website sales. It is calculated by dividing the total amount spent by the website purchases.

INSTAGRAM ANALYTICS

If you plan to exclusively use Instagram for your marketing campaigns, it is imperative to familiarize yourself with the app's Analytics page, where you can view and analyze the performance of your organic and boosted posts. When entering Analytics, make sure to review the following sections:

Content: Here you will find all of your boosted posts and Stories. Clicking on a post or Story will take you to its performance data, including number of views, likes, and shares. Visit this section if you want to see how your boosted posts and Stories are performing. If you want to see the data for your organic posts, visit your profile and click on the post you want to evaluate.

Activity: This section contains information about your profile activity, mainly the number of visits and website clicks it has received and the number of users it has reached (with data on impressions). Visit this section if you want to see how your account is performing.

Audience: This contains your followers' demographic information. It will show you a breakdown of your followers' locations, ages, and genders. Visit this page if you want to learn more about your audience. Use the information you find to inform your content strategy.

Note: If you are running ads on Instagram, your analytics will not appear in the Instagram app. It will appear in Business Manager.

FACEBOOK PAGE ANALYTICS

Facebook Insights keeps you updated on your pages' performance and allows you to view your followers' activity on your page. For example, you can view the data on your page's views, likes, and reach. When you visit your Facebook Insights page, you will see a list of subsections to the left.

Overview: Shows a summary of page activities from the last seven days. Information includes page views, page likes, reach, video views, and page followers.

Promotions: Allows you to create and buy promotions for four types of page objectives: increasing calls, increasing website visitors, increasing local awareness, and promoting your page. Think of promotions as ads for your page.

Followers: Provides data on the sources of your page follows and your total followers. The data for the latter can be broken down by unfollows, organic followers, paid followers, and net followers.

Likes: Provides data on page likes. You can view a benchmark report that compares your average likes over time, along with organic likes, paid likes, new likes, and unlikes. You can also view where your page likes occurred, and whether they occurred on your ads, your page, or on mobile.

Reach: Provides data on your posts' total reach and engagement.

Page Views: Provides data on total page views. You can view the age and gender of each individual who viewed your page; their country and city; the device the view occurred on; and the source of the view.

Actions on Page: Provides data on the total actions on your page, including clicks to get directions, to call, and to go to a website.

Posts: Provides data on your posts. You can view data on when your followers are online, which posts received the most engagement, and how much engagement each post received.

Events: Provides data on your events. You can view data on reach, views, engagement, ticket sales, and audience.

Videos: Provides performance insights on your videos. Information includes the minutes viewed and total video views.

People: Provides insights on your followers. Information includes age, gender, and country. You can also see which demographic engages more with your content.

Local: Provides insights on people within your location. Information includes activity and peak hours, demographics of people near you, and people near you who were reached by your ads.

Messages: Provides data on total conversations.

Instant Articles CTA: Provides data on CTAs in Instant Articles. Information includes total sign-ups, total impressions, sign-ups by age and gender, and sign-ups by location.

AFTERWORD

Before we part ways, I want to leave you with three pieces of advice.

First, keep your A/B tests simple. Test two things at a time. Do not overwhelm yourself.

Second, check your account every day. Facebook ads are like newborns. They require time and attention to survive. If you do not constantly watch your accounts, you will not be able to prevent the ROIs from plummeting.

Third, do not be afraid to make mistakes. When I started advertising on Facebook, a time when such a thing was still new, there were no resources to help me navigate through the platform. I had to master Facebook ads through trial and error. Do not penalize yourself too much when you make mistakes. Rather, learn from them and quickly fix any issue.

I hope this book has demystified the complexities of Facebook advertising, and I hope you pursue your endeavors as a Facebook advertiser. It is truly a revolutionary platform, and I wish you massive success with your campaigns.

UNLOCKING FACEBOOK'S HIDDEN AD TARGETING

Did you know that Facebook provides to certain advertisers hidden ad targeting options? These fields are not included in the targeting section of Ads Manager. Instead, they must be unlocked by a representative at Facebook or through a Facebook advertising agency like AdvertiseMint. An advanced resource for companies growing their Facebook ad campaigns, The Complete Guide to Hidden Facebook Ad Targeting includes more than 2,000 additional ad targeting options.

To download the printable version of this guide, visit the AdvertiseMint website at https://www.advertisemint.com/complete-guide-hidden-facebook-ad-targeting/.

GET SOCIAL

If, after reading this book, you still have burning questions that need answering, or if you find yourself stumped after dabbling with Facebook ads, do not hesitate to use the resources I provide in this book or to connect with me. There are a few ways we can get in touch:

1.   Connect through Social Media

Facebook: https://www.facebook.com/advertisemint

Instagram: https://www.instagram.com/advertisemint

Snapchat: https://www.snapchat.com/advertisemint

LinkedIn: https://www.linkedin.com/in/brianmeert

2.   The AdvertiseMint Facebook Group

You can join the AdvertiseMint Facebook group, where members discuss strategies and resolve issues together.

https://www.facebook.com/groups/advertisemint/

3.   Talk on Clarity

If you want one-on-one time with me to help you solve your problems, you can find me on Clarity.

www.clarity.fm/brianmeert

PROMOTIONS

Career Opportunities

Facebook advertising presents many career options, and not all of them are related to advertising and marketing. Here is a short list of career options you can pursue:

1. Facebook Ads Account Manager

If you love creating ads, managing accounts, talking to clients, and analyzing reports, then you will be happy and invigorated in the account manager position.

2. Sales Manager

Although you do not get to create ads and scale campaigns like account managers, you do get to talk about Facebook advertising to prospective customers. If you like connecting with people and flexing your persuasion skills, then you could pursue a career in sales. An advertising agency cannot exist without clients, and clients cannot connect with agencies without a sales team.

3. Graphic Designer

Ads, as you know by now, need to be refreshed every two weeks. But that cannot happen unless you have a dedicated graphic designer. If you love taking photos and editing them, then you can be a graphic designer. Graphic designers take photos, beautify them, or create something new for Facebook ads.

4. Video Editor

Many of my clients have content that needs to be reformatted for mobile—that is where a video editor comes in. Video editors often work with what they already have. They will receive videos that they can reformat for the right specs, videos that they can edit with music and text.

5. Photographer

Do you consider yourself a creative person? You can be one at a Facebook advertising agency. While some clients come to my agency with folders of media my team can use, some do not have any assets at all. This is where the photographer comes in. The photographer creates fresh content for clients every two weeks or per request.

6. Videographer

Videographers have a place in Facebook advertising, too. Because clients will need new videos several times a month, it is important to have a videographer on the team to produce fresh, original content.

7. Messenger Bot Developer

If clients want to create Messenger ads, they would need a chatbot to help them automate their responses to the customers who click on those ads. For this reason, a bot developer with technical and coding skills is often needed.

8. Customer Service Representative

Because Facebook ads all have a comments section, customers can easily respond to ads with complaints that the public can see. It is important that a dedicated customer service representative monitor the comments section and address all complaints. This keeps the company's image professional and trustworthy.

9. Copywriter

All ads must have copy, and who is better suited for the job than a talented copywriter? Copywriters have assignments nearly every day, creating copy for different brands. If you like variety in writing, then copywriting is the perfect fit for you.

10. Blogger

Advertising agencies often have a blog that contains posts related to their industries. My website, advertisemint.com, has a blog updated every day with news, how-to articles, guides, and advice related to social media, digital marketing, and digital advertising. The blog gives my company credibility and my website higher ranking for SEO.

11. CEO

Before I built my company, I worked as a freelance Facebook advertiser, helping clients scale their campaigns. A few years later, I hired account managers to help me manage my accounts. Bloggers, copywriters, salespersons, photographers, graphic designers, and video editors followed shortly thereafter. You can be the CEO of your company, too. You just need the skills, the drive, and an amazing team.

If you are looking for a career in Facebook advertising, and you want to be part of an amazing team, check out our company's career page at **https://www.advertisemint.com/careers/.**

ADVERTISEMINT PARTNER PROGRAM

The AdvertiseMint Partner Program incentivizes individuals, companies, or agencies to connect AdvertiseMint with clients who need advanced Facebook advertising management. The partner program offers 10% of revenue generated from the referred client for up to 12 months. You can learn more about the requirements for our partners program online at:

www.advertisemint.com/partners

GET THE LATEST NEWS ON FACEBOOK ADS

Facebook's advertising technology changes on almost a weekly basis. To keep updated on the latest changes, subscribe to AdvertiseMint's messenger bot, which sends you the best curated tips, tricks, and strategies to ensure your campaigns are successful. It is free to sign up. Visit **https://m.me/advertisemint** or scan the code below with your mobile phone camera.

MESSENGER BOT

Learning is a never-ending process. Even after you read this book, you still need to read everything you can about strategies and news related to Facebook advertising because things often change.

Strategies change, Facebook advertising products change, and customer behaviors change. If you want to be on top of the latest changes, subscribe to AdvertiseMint's Messenger bot, which will send you tips and advice related to Facebook ads.

AdvertiseMint Bot Link

https://m.me/advertisemint

SUBMIT YOUR PHOTO AND GET FEATURED

If you submit a photo of yourself with this book, you will be featured on this page. Here is how you do it: Post your photo on Instagram with the hashtag #facebookadsbook and tag @advertisemint. It is that easy.

VIDEOMINT

VIDEOMINT

If you need help generating creatives for your Facebook ad campaigns, sign up for VideoMint, a subscription service that produces amazing videos for you every month. Contact the number below if you are interested.

844-236-4686 ex. 2

GLOSSARY

A

A/B Testing

Also called split testing, this is a method advertisers use to test which ad elements, such as headlines, copy, images, calls to action, and targeting, work best on their target audience. A/B testing can help you compare the performance of multiple variables in a campaign and determine which one is best for your objectives.

Account Currency

The currency (e.g., dollar, peso, or euro) that an ad account uses. Any charges will appear in the selected currency.

Account ID

A unique ID for an ad account represented by a series of unique numbers. It may be needed if you are sharing access with your account or determining the difference between two accounts with the same name. You can find your ad account number in the dropdown menu located on the top left corner of Ads Manager.

Account Settings

An area of Facebook where you can view and edit account preferences. For example, you can edit your name and email address, notification preferences, and security features.

Account Spending Limit

The budget you set for your entire ad account. Your spending limit, which you can adjust at any time, is optional.

Actions

The data type that shows all actions taken by users within 24 hours after viewing an ad or sponsored story in a campaign. You will see this data only if you are promoting a page, event, or app. Actions include page and post likes, event RSVPs, and app installs.

Activity Log

The activity log, which only you can see, contains all the posts you posted or people posted on your timeline. Activity logs for pages are accessible only to those who manage the page.

Ad Account

The grouping of all your specific ad activity. Your ad account includes different campaigns, ad sets, ads, and billing information. You can manage multiple ad accounts through Business Manager.

Ad Auction

The method advertisers use to purchase ads. In the auction process, all Facebook ads compete against one another, and the ad with the best bid and value score wins.

Ad ID

This unique numerical ID differentiates between every ad created. This number is normally provided to Facebook's support team when asking for support for a problem.

Ad Reports

Ad reports contain all of the important metrics pertaining to your ad. Reports, which can be scheduled and saved for future use, can include date ranges, graphs, customized columns, and tables. Ad reports can be created or exported to ad accounts in Ads Manager.

Ad Set

All targeting for Facebook ads is done on the ad set level. An ad set can include multiple ads, bidding preferences, a budget, and a schedule. You can create an ad set for each of your audience segments by making the ads within the ad set target the same audience. This will help you control the amount you spend on each audience, decide when each audience will see your ads, and see metrics specific to each audience.

Ad Set Budget

The budget you set when you create an ad set. Two types of budgets exist: the daily budget and the lifetime budget. The daily budget is the maximum amount you are willing to spend each day, whereas the lifetime budget is the amount you are willing to spend for the duration of your campaign.

Ad Targeting

Ad targeting contains all of the target options you choose to define for your target audience (e.g., location, gender, age, likes, interests, relationship status, workplace, and education). All Facebook ads require you to create a target audience using its targeting options.

Add to Cart

The number of times an item was added to a shopping cart on your website because of your ad.

Add to Cart Conversion Value

The total value that represents the number of items that were added to a cart on your website because of your ad.

Admin

Admins are people who manage the activity of ad accounts, fan pages, or Facebook groups. Admins also have the ability to post, moderate, or control content and to add or remove other users from account roles.

Ads API

The Ads API allows you to create and manage ads programmatically on

Facebook. The API also allows Facebook Preferred Marketing Partners to build solutions for marketing automation with Facebook's advertising platform.

Ads Manager

The part of Business Manager where you can create ads and view, edit, and access performance reports for all of your campaigns, ad sets, and ads. You can also view all of your Facebook ad campaigns and payment history, change your bids and budgets, export ad performance reports, and pause or restart your ads at any time.

Advertising Policies

Facebook's advertising policies outline the dos and don'ts of Facebook advertising, listing the types of ads that are restricted or forbidden. Violation of Facebook's policies will result in blocked accounts or rejected ads.

Amount Spent

The total amount you have spent during the dates you have selected in Ads Manager.

App Install Ads

Facebook ads that urge users to install an app. Once clicked, the ad will direct users to the App Store or Google Play to install the app.

App Installs

The number of times users have installed your app because of your ad.

App Uses

The number of times users have used your app because of your ad.

Aquila Drone

Aquila is Facebook's first full-scale drone for Internet.org. Using a linked network of the drones, Facebook plans to use Aquila to provide internet access in remote parts of the world.

Audience

The group of people who can potentially see your ads.

Audience Insights

A Facebook tool designed to help marketers learn more about their target audience, including information about geography, demographics, lifestyle, and purchase behavior. With Audience Insights, advertisers can run reports on any Facebook user, including people connected to their fan page or people in a custom audience.

Audience Network

The Audience Network is a placement type that allows advertisers to place their ads in the apps and websites of Facebook's partners.

Audience Retention

A metric that measures the amount of time viewers are watching a video.

Augmented Reality (AR)

A technology that layers a digital image over a user's view of a physical, real-world environment. Unlike virtual reality (VR), which creates a digital 3D simulation of the real world, augmented reality augments the environment with graphic overlays and special effects.

Autobid

Also known as Optimized CPM, autobid is a setting that automatically optimizes bids to reach an advertising goal by adjusting spend to reach users who are most likely to complete a goal, whether that goal is impressions, clicks, app installs, or conversions.

Average Cost per Click (Average CPC)

The average cost per click for an ad.

Average Cost per Impression (Average CPM)

The cost incurred for every 1,000 impressions of an ad or for every 1,000 times an ad was displayed in front of a user.

Average Duration of Video Viewed

The average length of time people spent viewing a video. The average duration number is calculated by dividing the total video watch time by the play time.

Average Percent of Video Viewed

The average percentage of a video that people viewed. This number is calculated by dividing the total video view percentage by the total play time percentage.

B

Backup Payment Method

Additional optional payment methods that can be added to an ad account. If there is a problem with the primary payment method, Facebook will charge fees using the chosen backup payment method.

Bid

The amount advertisers pay to have an ad displayed on Facebook's platform.

Billing Summary

The billing summary lists all advertisers' past and current ad charges. Each summary will contain a description link that, when clicked, will reveal to advertisers a detailed breakdown for the charge, including the dates that the charge covers and the specific ads that ran during that period.

Billing Threshold

A billing method that bills an account after an advertiser has spent a certain amount. Billing thresholds vary by country, and they comply with an account's currency and payment method. Billing thresholds determine when and how often advertisers are billed for their ads.

Blocking

The action that allows Facebook users to block someone from communication. Once blocked, a user cannot search for or view the Facebook profile of another user, cannot add that user as a friend, and cannot send or receive messages from that user.

Boosted Post

A boosted post is a regular post that you pay Facebook to advertise. Boosted posts, like Facebook ads, will appear on the News Feeds of a target audience.

Broad Categories

The predefined targeting categories Facebook provides that groups users according to their likes and interests, the apps they use, and the pages they like, among other criteria.

Budget

The maximum amount you are willing to spend on each campaign.

Business Manager

A website that helps businesses and agencies manage their Facebook pages, ad accounts, and apps in one place. Business Manager also allows advertisers to centrally manage different permission levels of team members working on ad accounts or pages.

C

Call-to-Action Button (CTA Button)

The button that appears on a Facebook ad that takes users directly to a landing page. The button includes calls to action such as "shop now," "book now," "learn more," "sign up," "download," "shop more," "contact us," "apply now," and "donate now."

Campaign ID

A unique numerical ID associated with a campaign.

Campaign Level

The campaign level contains one or more ad sets and ads. When creating an ad at the campaign level, advertisers can choose an objective.

Campaign Spending Limit

A campaign spending limit allows advertisers to set an overall spending limit for an entire campaign. The limit stops all running ads once an account reaches the spending limit.

Canvas Ad

Canvas is an immersive Facebook ad that, once clicked, opens full screen in users' phones. Canvas ads can comprise videos, images, carousels, and CTA buttons, which users can swipe through, tilt for a panoramic view, or zoom in and out of.

Carousel Ad

Ads that include up to 10 images or videos within a single ad unit that direct users to specific locations on a website. Each Carousel Ad contains up to 10 carousel cards that users can swipe through and click.

Check-Ins

Check-ins is a Facebook feature that allows users to tag a business location in their posts. Only businesses that have a Facebook business page with an address entered in the page's profile can appear as options for check-ins.

Checkouts

The number of times a checkout was completed on a website because of an ad.

Checkouts Conversion Value

The total value returned from conversions on a website because of an ad. Advertisers must have custom conversions enabled for this value to appear in their reports.

Clicks

Clicks is a metric that is measured by the number of times a user clicks on an ad. Clicks to like, share, or comment, as well as clicks on the CTA button, are measured as clicks.

Clicks to Play

Clicks to play is a metric that measures the number of times a video starts and plays for a minimum of three seconds after a person has clicked it. This metric is available for videos uploaded and embedded directly to Facebook. It is not, however, available for links to videos that play off Facebook.

Clicks to Play Video

The number of clicks to play a video because of your ad. This will include all video views regardless of whether the video played for more than three seconds.

Click-Through Rate (CTR)

The number of clicks your ad receives divided by the number of times your ad is shown on the site (impressions) in the same time period.

Connections

Connections targeting is a targeting option in which advertisers can target or exclude the people who liked their page or location, installed their app, joined their event, used their app in the past 30 days, or checked in to their advertised location within 24 hours of viewing or clicking an ad or sponsored story.

Conversions

Conversions are the number of times people completed a desired action, such as purchases on a website or sign-ups for a newsletter.

Core Audiences

Core audiences is a targeting option that allows advertisers to reach precise audiences based on four main targeting types: location, demographic, interests, and behaviors. Facebook pulls data from the information users share on their profiles and the behaviors they exhibit online and offline.

Cost per Action

The average amount advertisers pay for each action users make on their ads. Payment costs depend on the number of advertisers competing to show their ads to their target audience. Well-designed ads will encourage more people to take action, and the more actions garnered for the budget, the lower the cost per actions will be.

Cost per All Actions

The average cost of all actions tracked by the Facebook pixel on a website after users viewed or clicked on an ad.

Cost per App Engagement

The average cost per action on an app because of an ad.

Cost per App Story Engagement

The average cost per action related to an app story because of an ad.

Cost per App Use

The average cost for each app use because of an ad.

Cost per Check-In

The average cost for each check-in because of an ad.

Cost per Checkout (Conversion)

The average cost for each checkout on a website because of an ad.

Cost per Click (CPC)

The amount advertisers pay each time a user clicks on their ads. The CPC for any ad is determined by the advertiser, and some advertisers may be willing to pay more per click than others. If advertisers bid on a CPC basis, they will be charged when users click on their ads and visit their websites. Total charges are based on the amount spent on the ad divided by all the clicks the ad received.

Cost per Clicks to Play Video

The cost calculated by the number of times users viewed 50% of your video, including views that skipped to that point.

Cost per Credit Spend Action

The average cost for each credit spend action because of an ad.

Cost per Event Response

The average cost for each user who joins an event because of an ad.

Cost per Gift Sale

The average cost of each gift sold on Facebook because of an ad.

Cost per Key Web Page View (Conversion)

The average cost for each view of a key page on a website because of an ad.

Cost per Lead (Conversion)

The average cost for each lead because of an ad.

Cost per Mobile App Achievement

The average cost for each level-achieved action in a gaming app because of an ad.

Cost per Mobile App Action

The average cost per action on an app because of an ad.

Cost per Mobile App (Add to Cart)

The average cost for each add-to-cart action in a mobile app because of an ad.

Cost per Mobile App (Add to Wish List)

The average cost for each add-to-wish-list action in a mobile app because of an ad.

Cost per Mobile App Checkout

The average cost for each checkout in an app because of an ad.

Cost per Mobile App Credit Spend

The average cost for each credit spend in an app because of an ad.

Cost per Mobile App Feature Unlock

The average cost for each feature or achievement unlocked in an app because of an ad.

Cost per Mobile App Install

The average cost for each app install because of an ad.

Cost per Mobile App Payment Detail

The average cost for each added payment information on an app because of an ad.

Cost per Mobile App Purchase

The average cost for each app purchase because of an ad.

Cost per Mobile App Rating

The average cost for each rating of an app because of an ad.

Cost per Mobile App Registration

The average cost for each registration in an app because of an ad.

Cost per Mobile App Search

The average cost for each search in an app because of an ad.

Cost per Mobile App Start

The average cost for each time a user starts an app because of an ad.

Cost per Mobile App (Tutorial Completion)

The average cost for each tutorial completed on an app because of an ad.

Cost per Offer Claim

The average cost for each offer claim because of an ad.

Cost per Other Mobile App Action

The average cost for other actions on an app because of an ad.

Cost per Other Website Conversion

The average cost for each time a user took another action on a website because of an ad.

Cost per Page Engagement

The average cost per engagement because of an ad.

Cost per Page Like

The average cost per page like because of an ad.

Cost per Page Mention

The average cost for each page mention as a result of an ad.

Cost per Page Tab View

The average cost per tab views on a page as a result of an ad.

Cost per Photo View

The average cost for each photo view as a result of an ad.

Cost per Post Comment

The average cost for each comment on a page's posts as a result of an ad.

Cost per Post Engagement

The average cost per engagement on a page's post as a result of an ad. This cost is calculated by dividing total spend by the total number of engagements.

Cost per Post Like

The average cost for each like on a page's post as a result of an ad.

Cost per Post Share

The average cost for each share on a page's post as a result of an ad.

Cost per Question

The average cost for each question follow-up as a result of an ad.

Cost per Registration (Conversion)

The average cost for each registration on a website as a result of an ad.

Cost per Thousand (CPM)

The average cost an advertiser pays for 1,000 impressions on an ad. If advertisers bid by CPM, they will be charged when users view their ads, regardless of whether they click on them.

Cost per Unique Click (All)

The cost per the number of clicks an ad receives. Cost per unique clicks is calculated by dividing the number of clicks an ad receives by the number of impressions.

Cost per Video View

The average cost per video view, which is calculated by dividing the amount spent by the number of video views.

Cost per Website Action (All)

The average cost per website action tracked by the Facebook pixel on a website after users viewed or clicked on an ad.

Cost per 10-Second Video View

The average cost per 10-second video view, calculated as the amount spent divided by the number of 10-second video views.

Cost per 1,000 People Reached

The average cost advertisers pay to show their ads to 1,000 unique users.

Cover Photo

The cover photo is the large picture at the top of a Facebook profile, right behind the profile picture. All cover photos are public: Anyone visiting a profile will be able to see it.

CPC (Link)

Cost per click to link is the amount charged each time someone clicks on a link in an ad that directs users off Facebook. Total charges are calculated by dividing the amount spent on the ad by the clicks to link.

Credit Spends

The number of times advertising coupons were spent in your app as a result of your ad.

Current Balance

The total amount spent on ads that have not been billed yet. This balance will clear automatically after Facebook charges the account. The summary of charges can be found in the billing section under Ads Manager.

Custom Audience

A Custom Audience is an ad-targeting option that allows advertisers to target an audience from an uploaded customer list. The list can comprise people from a customer file or people tracked by the Facebook pixel who have visited or taken actions on a website, app, or Facebook page.

Custom Conversions

Custom conversions allow advertisers to track and optimize for conversions without adding anything to the Facebook pixel code placed in a site. Custom conversions can be used with Standard Events or URL-based variables. Custom conversions replaced the Facebook conversion pixel, which was discontinued in 2016.

D

Daily Active Users

This is the number of people who have viewed or interacted with a Facebook page on a specific day, categorized by the type of action they perform.

Daily Budget

The amount you have indicated you are willing to spend on a specific campaign per day. Facebook will never charge you more than your daily budget on a given day. Each ad set will have a separate budget. Ads will automatically stop showing once a daily budget for the ad set has been met for that day.

Daily Page Activity

This data breaks down the different ways people engage with a Facebook page on a specific day. (Engagement does not include comments and likes on posts.) The daily page activity will show when followers post, upload photos or videos on a business page (if enabled), write reviews, or mention the page in posts posted on their walls or on their friends' walls.

Daily Spend Limit

The daily spend limit is the maximum amount Facebook allows advertisers to spend in one day.

Delivery

The delivery status indicates whether a campaign, ad set, or ad is currently running.

Delivery Fatigue

A phenomenon in which an ad's performance may decline after it has been running for extended periods of time.

Desktop App Credit Spends Conversion Value

The total value returned from advertising coupons spent in a desktop app as a result of an ad. This is based on the value assigned to the conversion type in the pixel code.

Destination

The ad's destination is the landing page that users will land on after they click on an ad.

Device

The device on which the conversion event you are tracking occurred. For example, if someone converted on a desktop computer, the device on analytics will appear as desktop.

Dynamic Product Ads

These ads help businesses sell products online by showing relevant products from their catalog to the people who want to buy them. Dynamic Product Ads give marketers a powerful set of tools to promote the right product to the right person at the right time, and with a personalized message.

E

End Date

The date a campaign is scheduled to stop. Campaigns can run continuously or until specific dates.

Event Responses

The number of RSVPs for an event as a result of an ad.

External Referrers

The number of views a Facebook page received from website URLs that are not part of Facebook.

F

Facebook Account Kit

The account kit helps users sign in to an app with their phone number or email address without the need for a password.

Facebook Analytics for Apps

Facebook Analytics for Apps provides analytics on developers' apps. The data includes information on audience insights such as age, gender, education, interests, country, language, and many more.

Facebook Audience Selector

The audience selector, a feature available to pages, allows page admins to select an audience for the content posted on the page.

Facebook Badge

A Facebook badge allows website owners to share their Facebook profiles, photos, or pages on their websites.

Facebook Event

Facebook event is a feature that lets users organize gatherings and respond to invites. Users can post statuses, upload photos, set dates, and enter event details to an event page.

Facebook Exchange (FBX)

The Facebook Exchange helps advertisers reach users who will potentially be interested in their offer. Interest is determined by the expressed interest in a similar type of offer online. This feature is typically used by advertisers who have data on users' intent to buy a product.

Facebook Friends

Facebook friends are people who are in a user's friends list on Facebook.

Facebook Lite

A version of Facebook that accommodates areas with low internet connectivity by using less data.

Facebook Live API

Facebook Live API allows device manufacturers to integrate Facebook Live directly into their latest video products. With the Live API, users can go beyond phone cameras and use Facebook Live on professional cameras, multi-camera setups, and programmatic sources such as games or screencasts.

Facebook Page

Facebook pages are profiles that represent businesses, public figures, and brands. Facebook pages look and function similarly to regular Facebook profiles, except they have several capabilities that profiles do not have, such as boosting and scheduling posts, creating ads, and targeting an audience.

Facebook Pixel

A piece of JavaScript code that tracks the actions and locations of users in a website.

Facebook Search

Facebook's search engine that helps users find people, posts, photos, places, pages, groups, apps, and events, among numerous other items.

Fan

In Page Insights and other places on Facebook, the term "fan" refers to the people who like or follow your page. These people are also referred to as followers.

Follow

A follow is an action that occurs when a user either likes or follows a page or a profile or adds another user as a friend. When a user follows a page or a person, that user will see the posts of the person or the page on News Feed.

Free Basics

A Facebook platform that provides free, basic access to websites that are otherwise difficult to access with basic internet services. Users can easily access information news related to maternal health, travel, local jobs, sports, communication, and the local government.

Frequency

The average number of times an ad was shown to each user.

Friends of Fans

A targeting option that allows advertisers to target individuals who are friends with people who follow or like the advertisers' pages.

G

Gift Sale Conversion Value

The total value returned from the gift sale conversions as a result of an ad.

Gift Sales

The number of gifts sold on Facebook as a result of an ad.

Groups

Facebook groups are private spaces where users can share interests and passions with other users who are not on their friends list. Users can post statuses and share documents, photos, and videos in groups. Currently, selling used items is the most popular use for Facebook groups.

I

Impressions

The number of times an ad is displayed on a user's screen.

Instagram Stories

Instagram Stories is a feature that allows users to share ephemeral, 24-hour videos and photos that vanish forever a day after the post was posted.

Instant Articles

Instant Articles is a Facebook feature that allows publishers' articles to quickly and easily load and open within its app. Instant Articles is also a placement option for Facebook ads.

Interest Targeting

Interest targeting is a targeting option that allows advertisers to target an audience with particular interests such as activities, music, movies, and TV shows.

K

Key Web Page Views (Conversion)

The number of times users viewed a key page on a website as a result of an ad.

L

Landing Page

A landing page is a single web page that users arrive to after clicking an ad.

Lead Ad

A lead ad, a Facebook ad type, is a digital form that collects users' information. Lead ads are typically used to collect contact information to grow leads. The most common information collected are first and last name, phone number, and email address.

Lead Magnet

A valuable offer advertisers give to potential customers in exchange for their personal information.

Leads (Conversion)

A lead is a potential customer who responded to a lead ad and gave the advertiser his or her contact information. When data is being analyzed, it can also refer to the number of new leads acquired as a result of an ad.

Leads Conversion Value

The total value returned from acquiring new leads as a result of an ad.

Lifetime Budget

A lifetime budget is the amount advertisers spend over the lifetime of an ad set.

Like

Liking is an action that occurs on Facebook when users click on the Like button, symbolized by Facebook's thumbs-up icon.

Like Sources

A metric found in Page Insights that shows the number of times users liked a Facebook page within a specified date range.

Liked by Page

A section on Facebook that features all of the other pages that another page liked.

Link Ads

Link ads contain CTA buttons that direct users to a website.

Link Clicks

The number of link clicks on an ad or page that direct users off Facebook as a result of an ad (e.g., clicks to install an app, to view an off-site video, and to visit another website).

Lookalike Audiences

An audience that closely resembles a target audience. Advertisers create Lookalike Audiences by uploading a Custom Audience to Facebook.

M

Marquee Campaigns

A premium product for Instagram advertisers that helps drive mass awareness and expand reach in a short period of time. Advertisers usually use marquee campaigns for movie premieres and product launches.

Media Consumption

The number of times users clicked and viewed media content advertisers published on their pages on a specific day.

Messenger

A Facebook standalone app that lets users send instant messages to friends.

Messenger Bots

AI technology that functions as an automated response tool for businesses with Facebook pages.

Mixed Values

In Ads Manager and Power Editor, mixed values, also known as multiple values, indicate that a value for a field is not identical across the campaigns, ad sets, or ads an advertiser is editing.

Mobile App Achievements

The number of levels achieved in a mobile app as a result of an ad.

Mobile App Actions

The number of actions that occurred in a mobile app as a result of an ad.

Mobile App Actions Conversion Value

The total value returned from actions that occurred in a mobile app as a result of an ad.

Mobile App Add-to-Cart

The number of times customers added an item to a shopping cart in a mobile app as a result of an ad.

Mobile App Adds-to-Cart Conversion Value

The total value returned from items added to a cart in an app as a result of an ad. The value is based on the value assigned to the conversion type in the pixel code.

Mobile App Adds-to-Wish-List

The number of times something was added to a wish list in an app as a result of an ad.

Mobile App Adds-to-Wish-List Conversion Value

The total value returned from items added to a wish list in an app as a result of an ad. This is based on the value assigned to the conversion type in the pixel code.

Mobile App Checkouts

The number of checkouts initiated in an app as a result of an ad.

Mobile App Checkouts Conversion Value

The total value returned from checkouts initiated in a mobile app as a result of an ad. This is based on the value assigned to the conversion type in the pixel code.

Mobile App Content Views

The number of content views in an app as a result of an ad.

Mobile App Content Views Conversion Value

The total value returned from content views in a mobile app as a result of an ad. This is based on the value assigned to the conversion type in the pixel code.

Mobile App Credit Spends

The number of times advertising coupons were spent in a mobile app as a result of an ad.

Mobile App Feature Unlocks

The number of features, levels, or achievements users unlocked in a mobile app as a result of an ad.

Mobile App Payment Details

The number of times payment information was entered in a mobile app as a result of an ad.

Mobile App Purchases

The number of times users purchased in an app as a result of an ad.

Mobile App Purchases Conversion Value

The total value returned from purchases made in a mobile app as a result of an ad. This is based on the value assigned to the conversion type in the pixel code.

Mobile App Ratings

The number of ratings in a mobile app as a result of an ad.

Mobile App Ratings Conversion Value

The total value returned from ratings in a mobile app as a result of an ad. This is based on the value assigned to the conversion type in the pixel code.

Mobile App Registrations

The number of mobile app registrations as a result of an ad.

Mobile App Searches

The number of searches in a mobile app as a result of an ad.

Mobile App Starts

The number of mobile app starts as a result of an ad.

Mobile App Tutorial Completions

The number of tutorials completed in an app as a result of an ad.

Monthly Active Users

This is the number of people who viewed or interacted with a Facebook page during the previous 30 days.

Multicultural Affinity

In targeting, this is a term that describes users who are interested in and likely to respond well to multicultural content. Targeting is based on affinity, not ethnicity.

N

Native Advertising

On Facebook, native advertising is a type of disguised online advertising in which marketers create ads that match the look, tone, and function of regular, unpaid posts.

Net Likes

The difference between the number of people who have liked a page and the number of people who have unliked a page over a specific time period.

New Likes

The total number of unique users who liked a Facebook page during a specific time period.

News Feed

News Feed, a scrollable trail of posts, is the main part of Facebook where the posts of friends, family, followed pages, and ads appear.

Notes

A feature that lets users publish messages in rich-text format.

Notifications

Updates about activity on Facebook that a user is involved in. For example, users can receive notifications if someone commented on their posts or a post that they previously commented on. They can also receive reaction, birthday, and saved post notifications, among many others.

O

Objective

The goal for a Facebook ad. Objectives include traffic, engagement, lead generation, and video views, among numerous others.

Offer

A discount or digitized coupon code users can claim from a Facebook ad.

Offer Claimed Story

A sponsored story highlighting users who have claimed a Facebook offer.

Offer Claims

The number of claims on an offer as a result of an ad.

Optimizing for App Events

An optimization and pricing option available in Power Editor and Ads API for mobile app engagement ads. It optimizes an ad for users most likely to complete an app event.

Organic Reach

Organic reach is the number of unique individuals who saw a specific post from a page on their News Feeds or from the page itself.

Other Clicks

A metric that measures clicks on page titles to see more, not clicks on a page's content.

Other Mobile App Actions

The number of other actions in a mobile app as a result of an ad.

Other Website Conversion Value

The total value returned from other conversions on a website as a result of an ad.

Other Website Conversions

The number of other conversions on a website as a result of an ad.

P

Page Admin

The highest role assigned for a Facebook page. Page admins have the most capabilities, from assigning new roles and changing page settings to adding or removing other page contributors.

Page Engagement

The number of engagements on a page and a page's posts as a result of an ad.

Page Like Story

A sponsored story that features users who liked a page.

Page Likes

The number of likes on a page as a result of an ad.

Page Mentions

The number of mentions of a page as a result of an ad.

Page Post Ad

A regular post from a page that an advertiser turns into an ad in Ads Manager or Power Editor.

Page Post Sponsored Story

An ad that promotes the interaction (i.e., like or comment) of a target user's friend with the advertiser's page post.

Page Roles

A function assumed by a person managing a Facebook page. Roles include admin, editor, moderator, advertiser, and analyst.

Page Tab Views

The number of tab views on a page as a result of an ad.

Page Tabs

Buttons that mark pages that users can click and open.

Page Views

The total number of times users viewed a Facebook page during a period of time.

Paid Reach

This is the number of unique individuals who saw a specific post from a page through a paid source such as a Facebook Ad or Promoted Post.

Partner Categories

Targeting options that Facebook's third-party partners provide. The targeting options under partner categories are taken from third-party data on offline behaviors.

Payment Methods

Verified forms of payment added to an ad account.

People Taking Action

The number of unique users who took an action (e.g., liking a page or installing an app) as a result of an ad.

Photo Views

The number of photo views as a result of an ad.

Pixel Helper

A Chrome extension that helps advertisers check whether their Facebook pixel is working properly on any website.

Placement

The location where ads will appear. Placements include desktop News Feed, mobile News Feed, and Audience Network, among many others.

Post Comments

The number of comments on a page's posts as a result of an ad.

Post Engagement

The number of actions (i.e., likes, comments, shares, photo views, link clicks, and video views) related to a page's posts as a result of an ad.

Post Feedback

The number of likes and comments on posts published from a page during the time period selected.

Post Reach

This is the number of people who have seen a post. A post counts as reaching someone when it is shown in their News Feed. Figures displayed in Insights are for the first 28 days after a post was created and include people viewing the post on desktop and mobile.

Post Shares

The number of post shares as a result of an ad.

Post Views

The number of times a story published on your Facebook page News Feed was viewed during the time period you select.

Posts to Page

Posts to page are posts posted on a page by someone other than an admin.

Potential Reach

The number of monthly active people on Facebook that match the audience defined through audience-targeting selections.

Power Editor

Power Editor is a page within Business Manager that allows advertisers to simultaneously edit multiple ads at once.

Primary Payment Method

The default payment method for an ad account.

Profile

Facebook users' personal pages that detail their personal information, posting activity, and interactions with other users. Profiles, which cannot be used for commercial use, can either be public or private.

Project ARIES

Project ARIES (Antenna Radio Integration for Efficiency in Spectrum) is a terrestrial system focused on improving the speed, efficiency, and quality of internet connectivity around the world. It provides a consistent, high-bandwidth internet experience to both developing and developed economies that can suffer from insufficient data rates.

R

Reach

The total number of users who saw an advertiser's ad.

Registrations (Conversion)

The number of times users registered on a website as a result of an ad.

Registrations Conversion Value

The total value returned from completed registrations on a website as a result of an ad.

Relevance Score

The relevance score estimates an ad's relevance to its target audience in real time.

Reports

Reports are the documentation of the most important ad metrics that show how an advertiser is reaching his or her business goals.

Result Rate

The number of results received divided by the number of impressions.

Results

The number of actions as a result of an ad. The results shown are based on the objective.

S

Social Click Rate

The number of social clicks divided by social impressions.

Social Clicks

Clicks on ads displayed to users as social proof.

Social Clicks (All)

The number of clicks on ads (i.e., likes, reactions, and shares) displayed to users as social proof.

Social Impressions

The number of times an ad that highlighted its engagement was displayed in front of users.

Social Plug-ins

Buttons that users can install into their websites. The buttons allow users to share their experiences off Facebook with their friends on Facebook. Clicking the share-to-Facebook button from a website to share an article is one example.

Social Reach

The number of users who saw an ad that highlighted its engagement.

Source Audience

A source audience is an audience advertisers derive their Lookalike Audience from. Page fans and Custom Audience are examples of a source audience.

Start Date

The day a campaign starts.

Status

The current state of ad sets and ads. Ads can show a status of on, off, running, paused, completed, or deleted.

Suggested Bid Range

A bid range that Facebook suggests to advertisers to ensure that their ads receive the right amount of impressions.

T

Tagging

An action that links a person or page to something a user posts, whether that is a photo, a status, or a check-in.

Ten-Second Video Views

The number of times users have viewed your video for 10 seconds. If your video is less than 10 seconds, then this refers to the number of times people viewed 97% of your video.

Thirty-Second Video Views

The number of times users have viewed your video for 30 seconds. If your video is 30 seconds or less, then this refers to the number of times people viewed 97% of your video.

Ticker

The ticker is a bar on the right side of Facebook desktop that updates users of their friends' activities in real time.

Timeline

The timeline, located front and center on a Facebook profile, is a scrollable trail of posts that a user or a friend of a user posted. Tagged posts and life events also appear on the timeline.

Timeline Review

A privacy setting that allows a user to approve or reject posts that they have been tagged in or posts that friends want to post on the user's timeline.

Top Stories

Top stories, which Facebook's algorithm thinks are relevant to a user, appear on top of a user's News Feed. Posts that have a high score in Facebook's algorithm will appear higher in News Feed.

Total Conversion Value

The total revenue returned from conversions or Facebook credit spends that occurred on a website or an app. This is based on the value assigned to the conversion type in the pixel code.

Trademark

A trademark is a word, slogan, symbol, or logo that identifies and distinguishes the products or services offered by one party from those offered by others.

Trending

A small box on the right side of Facebook desktop that features a list of topics that have recently spiked in popularity on Facebook.

U

Unique Clicks (All)

The total number of unique users who clicked on an ad. For example, if 10 people click on the same ad 5 times, the ad will have 10 unique clicks.

Unique CTR (All)

A value calculated by dividing the number of people who clicked anywhere in an ad by the number of people reached. For example, if an ad that was shown to 1,000 users received 10 unique clicks, the unique CTR would be 1%.

Unlikes

In analytics, the number of unique users who unliked a page during a specified date range.

Unpublished Page Post

An unpublished page post, also known as a dark post, is a post created in Power Editor that will not immediately appear in News Feed and pages. This allows advertisers to create an ad for that post without publishing it to the public.

V

Verification Hold

A temporary charge on an advertiser's account used to validate a credit card. The $1.01 charge will be removed from the credit card within three to five business days.

Verified Page

A Facebook page that has been verified by Facebook as authentic. Verified pages contain a check mark alongside their names.

Video Ads

Video ads are ad formats that, when clicked, play a video.

Video Views

The number of times users viewed a video for three seconds or more.

Video Views to 25%

The number of times users viewed a video to 25% of its length, including views that skipped to that point.

Video Views to 50%

The number of times users viewed a video to 50% of its length, including views that skipped to that point.

Video Views to 75%

The number of times users viewed a video to 75% of its length, including views that skipped to that point.

Video Views to 95%

The number of times users viewed a video to 95% of its length, including views that skipped to that point.

Viral Reach

Viral reach is the number of unique users who saw a page post from a story published by one of their Facebook friends.

Virtual Reality

Technology that creates an immersive, simulated 3D environment.

W

Website Action Value (All)

The total value of the actions tracked by a Facebook pixel on a website after users clicked an ad.

Website Actions (All)

The total number of actions tracked by a Facebook pixel on a website after users clicked the ad.

ABOUT THE AUTHOR

Brian Meert is the CEO of AdvertiseMint, the leading agency specializing in Facebook advertising. With more than 15 years of digital marketing experience, Brian founded AdvertiseMint after Facebook launched Ads Manager, and he saw its potential as an advertising channel.

Brian began his digital advertising career in college, using his cafeteria money to run paid search ads for a start-up business. He completed his MBA in marketing and quickly moved to Hollywood to pursue entertainment marketing. He founded and sold Gofobo.com, a ticketing system for movie screenings now used by Disney, Warner Bros, and Paramount Pictures.

When Brian is not monitoring Facebook ads, talking to clients, or holding team meetings, he enjoys CrossFit, wakeboarding, hiking, and spending time at the beach. You will often find him teaching workshops on Facebook advertising, where he met his wife, Maricia, who also works in social media. An avid traveler, Brian has lived in Fiji, Australia, and Greece.